50 Ways To Love Your Lover

Are you ready

for your

greatest adventure

in romance

and relationship?

50 Ways To Love Your Lover

50 Ways To Love Your Lover

50 Ways To Love Your Lover

Copyright © 2013-2024 by Barry S. Selby.

All rights reserved. No part of this book may be reproduced or transmitted in any form without permission in writing from the author, except by a reviewer who may quote brief passages for review purposes.

ISBN: 978-0989885201

First printing, December 2013
Revised and Updated, May 2023
Updated, April 2024

"*50 Ways To Love Your Lover* skillfully and eloquently guides the reader into the discovery that we have direct access to the love and happiness we long for. Full of practical wisdom and inspired insight."

Michael Bernard Beckwith
author of **Life Visioning**

"Barry Selby's book, *50 Ways to Love your Lover* is a beautifully written, inspirational and practical guide for bringing more joy, life and love into our relationships. Barry shows us the power we have as individuals to actually be the source of and the cause of the joy in our relationships."

Julie Ferman
Award Winning Matchmaker
Founder of **CupidsCoach.com**

50 Ways To Love Your Lover

This book is dedicated

to lovers everywhere.

To my ex-lovers,

to your ex-lovers,

and to you.

May you find value,

transformation and healing

in these pages,

and may your love life

be forever transformed,

as you go forward in life.

50 Ways To Love Your Lover

Contents

Acknowledgements xix

Introduction.. xxv

50 Ways To Love Your Lover 1

ABOUT YOUR SELF

#1 It Is An Inside Job 5

#2 Honor Yourself, They Will Too 11

#3 True Romance Requires Giving Your Heart.................17

#4 Know Your Core Values..23

#5 Surrender To Your Greatest Possibility 29

#6 Are You Alone, Or Lonely? There's A Difference 35

ABOUT YOUR HISTORY

#7   Objects In The Mirror Closer Than They Appear 45

#8   Your Baggage Is Never Caused By Your New Relationship 51

#9   Stop Projecting Childhood Experience On Your Partner............... 61

#10 It Is Not Your Job To Forgive Your Partner 69

#11 If You Love Your Partner More Than Yourself, Why? 83

#12 Lovers Come And Go. You Are The Constant 89

ABOUT YOUR JOURNEY

#13 Real Education Happens In Relationship 97

#14 Freedom Is A Primary Quality... 103

#15 There's Always More To Have In Romance 109

#16 Love In 3D (Depth).. 115

| #17 | Relationships Are Like Rubber Bands | 121 |
| #18 | Relationship Is A Spiritual Practice | 127 |

ABOUT YOUR PARTNER

#19	Never Presume You Know Everything	135
#20	Give More Than The Other, From Your Overflow	141
#21	Listen To Your Partner, Hear What They Truly Say	147
#22	Want Something From Your Partner?	153
#23	Cherish, Worship, Honor & Respect Your Partner	159
#24	Be Your Partner's Biggest Cheerleader	165

ABOUT AUTHENTICITY & COMMUNICATION

| #25 | Difference Between Codependence & Interdependence | 173 |
| #26 | Telepathy Rarely Works | 181 |

#27	Failure In Communication Includes	187
#28	He Said, She Said Is Pointless, No One Wins	193
#29	Being Honest Changes, Moment To Moment	199
#30	If You Blame Your Partner, You Will Lose	205

ABOUT LOVE & ROMANCE

#31	Relationship Rebound Is A Disservice	213
#32	Love From Your Overflow	219
#33	True Romance Is Sacred, Profound And A Pleasure	225
#34	Love And Chemistry And Sex	231
#35	Love Is The Best Lubricant Ever Created	239
#36	Be Romantic. How To?	245

ABOUT SEXUAL ATTRACTION

#37 Men and Women Attract Each Other Differently **253**

#38 We Carry Both Masculine And Feminine Energy.........................**259**

#39 Connect And Express Your Authentic Nature **267**

#40 Ladies, Let Your Man Be Masculine...**275**

#41 Gentlemen, Do Your Ladies A Favor **281**

#42 Men Will Never Understand Women **287**

ABOUT LIFE & THE WORLD

#43 Don't Trade Your Friends & Your Life For Your Lover................**295**

#44 Live Your Purpose, Share Your Gifts **301**

#45 Take A Trip Together Within The Early Months **307**

#46 Do You Have Deal-Breakers? **313**

#47 Know What Is Important To You..**319**

ABOUT YOUR FUTURE

#48 If You Don't Know Where You're Going **327**

#49 Have A Vision Of Your Ideal Romance? **333**

#50 Choose Your Beloved Intentionally **341**

About The Author **347**

Bibliography **353**

Get More **357**

50 Ways To Love Your Lover

Acknowledgements

This book was birthed from my own learning, my own journey through relationships, from my study of many, many couples, and clients, and from the wisdom and guidance of many teachers.

I discovered and created the majority of these 50 principles from the pain and loss caused by NOT living them in my past relationships. This pain, more than anything else, drove me into my own study and healing journey, and which led to the book you now hold in your hands.

First, I acknowledge and dedicate this book to my parents, not just because without them, I would not be here (obvious, I know!), but also because of their example of commitment and loving marriage that spanned almost 60 years. They provided me with lessons and patterns that I see in my own life. Both parents have transitioned, my mother in 2012, and my father in 2021. Their memory and lessons still persist with me.

I'll speak more about them (and my early love life) in the Introduction.

I have had good fortune to experience powerful transformation and education in workshops, trainings and seminars, and with master facilitators, authors and teachers. I continue to study and learn (that's a tip, by the way), and trust that the integration, distillation and interpretation of what I learn and share with you has value and impact in your life too.

50 Ways To Love Your Lover

I am grateful to so many people, including, most definitely, the ladies I have loved. A couple of these relationships were catalysts (to put it mildly) that ultimately launched me into the work that I live now – the teaching, coaching and facilitation that comes with the affectionate title of "The Love Doctor," given to me by my clients and friends.

I am also grateful to my teachers, my coaches, my guides, and friends who supported me, cajoled me, occasionally slapped me upside the head, and generally kept me on track to get here. I appreciate all of you.

Some individuals supported and inspired me consciously, and some individuals had no idea they were so powerfully assisting me on my path. To you all, I am grateful.

I have listed a few here, in no particular order; please know there are many more supporters and catalysts than these select few.

David Boufford is a good friend, and a very astute business strategist, who has, on more than one occasion, been my go-to guy for business strategy, clarity, and more than occasional tough-love coaching.

Thank you for always being a resource, stalwart friend, and reminder of the joy in life. His mastery as business strategist is only matched by his inspirational work as his alter ego Mr. Positive. You can find him at **mrpositive.com**.

Brad Axelrad is another good friend, business coach and powerhouse leader, who gave me my first brand (The Passion Consultant) which has evolved though it still defines and transforms me.

Thank you, Brad, for your friendship and counsel. I am always glad to return the favor. He is a powerfully loving coach, business consultant (and one helluva car driver!). Find Brad at **bradaxelrad.com**.

Rikk Galvan, who truly was the person who started this whole book process for me. His marketing insight and genius guided me to share what I believe and have learned about relationships and romance in a series of daily social media posts that initially were just a way to share my guidance for others, and to invite client interest.

Yet, as soon as they were out on the web for all to see, it became crystal clear these were to become the basis for this book you now have in your hands. Thank you Rikk, for starting the wheels in motion, even though neither one of us knew where it would end up. If your company is in need of great marketing, Rikk is your man – **linkedin.com/in/rikkgalvan**.

There are many more individuals along my path, some who gave more than I expected, some who supported me more than they know. Some have been teachers by example, and some have been teachers by calling, and have shown me the next piece of the puzzle, the next step toward this goal.

I thank my many friends and co-conspirators who have been fellow travelers and guides on this road. I am grateful for your gifts and support for my journey to this point and to the release of this book.

I trust you will find value in these pages, and inspiration, insight and recognition in these **50 Ways To Love Your Lover**, which are truly principles for a healthy and happy relationship.

I invite you to take these principles to heart, to own them for yourself, and to embody them so they become automatic in your daily life, such that your romance and love blossom and grow continually.

Enjoy this journey.

50 Ways To Love Your Lover

Introduction

Over many years, and through many partnerships in romance, both my own and of those around me, I have recognized there is a whole lot more to relationships that just two people getting together.

Yes, that may appear obvious and trite, however what exactly makes or breaks a relationship has fascinated me and certainly changed me over the years too.

Yet that wasn't how I always saw things. Early on, I believed it only took a small spark between two people and the magic would take care of the rest. It is a common myth that many people still believe.

Yes, I was an incurable romantic (OK, I still am, somewhat), and saw love through rose-tinted glasses.

I had evidence to support the belief, that it was easy and simple. At least, I believed so.

My parents, according to my observations, only needed to love each other and everything worked, simple as that. They had a smooth marriage as far as I saw, for almost 60 years in fact.

That didn't work so well in my own early dating experiences. Early romantic relationships ended painfully and usually abruptly.

50 Ways To Love Your Lover

The simple conclusion I made (that I know other people have made and still make) was to believe I chose my romance partners poorly. None of these girls or women, obviously, was the perfect match for me. I was certainly not experiencing my parents' demonstration of stability and durability in relationship with the women I dated.

One key piece of information I should disclose: I had taken on a belief about my parents that they didn't intentionally teach me. According to my memory (which is not photographic by the way), my parents didn't argue or have upsets during my childhood and growing years.

Whether they did or didn't get upset with each other wasn't relevant. What impacted my relationship experience was what I took on as my belief, which was love and upset didn't mix. I believed we fall in love and live happily ever after, pure and simple.

However, it wasn't (and isn't) that simple. Let me run through that again.

As I said, I had taken on this belief from my parents, even though they hadn't instructed me or intentionally taught me this. I simply didn't recall them ever arguing, or showing any signs of temper or upset in front of me, at least according to my own memory. Yet, from this perceived experience, I made up the logical belief for myself that said "relationships are always loving and never experience upset or argument."

My relationships in my teens and early twenties didn't live up to that rather stratospheric rule, and you would be right to guess these early relationships didn't last very long either.

In fact, each and every early romance ended abruptly for me, the moment there was an argument, upset, or anger. At that moment I shut down, broke up with my girlfriend, or simply left, leaving her even more upset and probably confused as well.

I believed love could not co-exist with discord, anger, upset or disagreement. In my early dating life, if ... actually ... *when* I had an argument with my girlfriend (or she with me), I believed the love must be gone, so I left. That was the logical path I followed. Not once, but repeatedly.

I didn't know about make-up sex, so I really missed out. OK, that was meant to be a joke, however the truth was (and is) not so funny. I lost out on romance and a deeper relationship.
I didn't know any better, which is true for so many of us.

According to my young memory, my parents never got angry, upset, or disagreed in any way with each other. That was the way I saw them, and even if occasionally they did show upset, I ignored that as it did not match my perception and would have violated my view of them and of their relationship.

Thus, my own relationships could only be successful if there was no upset, discord, etc., with my girlfriend. You can probably guess that every one of my young relationships ultimately never worked out, and you'd be right. It took more than a few discordant endings like this to wake me up to consider a different possibility.

Every one of us, yes you too, has taken on beliefs and rules from our parents about relationships and how they work. We don't necessarily learn from what our parents and adult role models say, rather we more readily learn from their behavior that we witness. We learn about relationships (like most things in life) from how our parents act, and what they do, rather than what they say. This is a vital and key distinction.

50 Ways To Love Your Lover

We adopt beliefs about what we *perceive* to be the way things are, not necessarily the actual way it is. This could be a paradigm shift for you. It may change your understanding of how you see your own relationships.

In my own history, I clearly demonstrated that, according to my rules, arguing and love could not co-exist in the same relationship. Each budding romance would end abruptly if there was any discord, difference of opinion, or heaven forbid, an argument. *Because that would have violated my beliefs about relationships.*

This was the beginning of my journey, so to speak.

This experience was part of my personal emotional and mental baggage from my past that I dragged from relationship to relationship, repeating the same experience over and over again.

You have likely done the same – you learned behaviors, beliefs and patterns of relationship from the adults you grew up with and around, and that became the baggage that you also carry (or drag) with you from each past relationship to your next one.

These deep-seated rules and beliefs become automatic for almost everyone, and it often takes many relationship mishaps, break-ups and pain before a change is made, if ever.

Did your parents give you a relationship manual when you were a kid? I know I wasn't. I also didn't have Romance 101 as a selectable course at high school or even college. I suspect you didn't either. It always strikes me as odd that we did have sex education in school, yet no relationship education. Things that make you go hmmmm?

There is hope, however. You're reading this book, which will help you change your journey. I wouldn't claim this to be the book you never had in high school, though I believe it will fill in some gaps in your education.

This book is a work of love, a reference, a compendium, a gathering of principles that I believe make relationship a wonderful place to live, love and grow.

Some of the principles in this book will help you understand your past, your upbringing, and your self-defined relationship paradigm with your parents which will show you how you got to where you are (that baggage mentioned earlier).

Other principles will shed light on your future vision for relationship, and there are even principles that will show you ways of deepening the love you already have, to restore the flame that may have flickered, and almost disappeared, and other principles explain some interesting insights on sexual attraction. That should hold your attention.

This book gathers many core principles, inspirations and insights from my own experience, study and learning, and is a powerful and, hopefully, entertaining starting point from which to have phenomenal romance and amazing love relationships.

This book covers a gamut of relationship principles which will help you have a shift in your own experience, and a definite transformation of your relationship paradigm, whether the one you are in now, or if you are single, your next one.

These principles are not simply suggestions. If followed, these teachings will guide you to a much greater joy and love in romance, and a transformed journey of love and relationship.

If you don't follow these principles, I can't be held responsible for your relationship mistakes or loneliness. You have been warned.

These are not the *only* principles. That would be way too presumptuous. However, don't dismiss or treat these as simply *suggestions* or *tips*, they are much more than that. Calling them simply *tips* would be like calling a Siberian tiger a housecat!

These principles are gathered here to give you direct guidance, options and steps that can absolutely transform your relationship experience into something magical and immensely satisfying.

These are categorically honest, simple, and workable tools that, if applied, will change how you experience romance, how you love your partner, and perhaps most importantly, how you treat and love yourself.

This book is a reference, a journey of awakening and transformation, and a workbook for your study and guidance. There are worksheets and online support available as well – more on that in a moment.

This book is also a resource filled with provocative ideas, rather than a flowing story just for your entertainment, although I hope you will be entertained as well as educated. You might read this book front to back, or choose specific chapters based on what pulls your interest.

You could take each Chapter for a test-drive, for a week, to meditate on it, journal about it, and perhaps see how you can live it for that week. With 50 principles applied this way, it would certainly be a transformational year.

These 50 principles are useful to you if you are single or in relationship, if you want to deepen your relationship, or if you know you need a transformation in how you participate in relationship. If you are male or female, you will find value, inspiration, growth opportunities and more. They are each worthy of review and deliberation as you go about your days and live your life.

I invite you to keep a pen and highlighter handy. You might also find a notepad or journal useful to write about what you discover, uncover, resolve, and release while you read. I have provided Notes pages between the chapters, intentionally, to also assist with your reflection and journaling.

As I mentioned, there are supplemental worksheets available for specific Chapters to help you succeed, as well as suggestions for next steps and additional tools. You'll find indicators along the way.

Use these relationship and romance principles to make a truly positive impact in your life and transform how you go about being in relationship, how you attract your heart's desire, and how you treat yourself whether you are single or in relationship.

I appreciate you taking the time to read this book, to consider these 50 principles for your life, and to take conscious steps to have better and more fulfilling relationships. You are a rare individual to do so, and I acknowledge your courage.

Congratulations, by the way. Your intention, and your reading of this book to this point, has already changed the course of your love-life for the better.

So, without further ado, let's begin at the beginning, with the first principle.

50 Ways To Love Your Lover

50 Ways
To Love
Your Lover

50 Ways To Love Your Lover

ABOUT YOUR SELF

50 Ways To Love Your Lover

#1

If you are looking for someone else to fulfill you, you will never be fulfilled. Hint: It is an inside job.

Our society teaches us we need each other, that when we find that someone, we will be complete. In the movies (and love songs), you hear phrases like "You complete me," "I can't live without you," and the tragic "Don't leave me, I'll die without you."

There are literally millions of co-dependent love-songs over the airwaves, co-dependent romance movies and co-dependent shows on TV.

Yes, we are trained, or more accurately entrained, to believe and expect that we will find our satisfaction and fulfillment, by looking outside of ourselves. This becomes our belief as well. And our love-life is no different.

Many people have based their lives, their relationships, and their choices on what they see and hear from around them, such as the aforementioned movies, shows and songs.

50 Ways To Love Your Lover

Here's a cold hard fact for you (like a bucket of ice-water perhaps): Your partner will never fully satisfy your every need, want and desire, all the time. Never.

There is another choice.

In fact, there is only **one** other choice, and it is one that more and more people are waking up to and realizing for themselves.

If you are reading this book, I suspect you are seeking a different choice, a healthier choice, an intentional choice.

This different choice is the choice of loving yourself, loving who you are, what you are about, independent of anyone, or anything, else.

As you love yourself authentically, and honestly, you will discover something magical happens.

You will discover that you don't need anyone else at all.

There is no soulmate out there who will complete you or make you whole. Sorry to break it to you. In fact, your soulmate (if you believe in such things) cannot be with you and will likely not even recognize or find you (or you them), until you understand and live this.

As you become more self-sufficient and self-fulfilled, you will recognize that what attracts you in another is how much love you can share in overflow with them.

This will automatically occur, as they also love from their overflow.

Sharing love this way is abundant and effortless, and you will discover new and deeper ways of being with another that you never knew before.

And you will find another sort of love song to enjoy.

Yes, you have that to look forward to, as you trust this practice and grow in your own self-fulfilling love.

As mentioned earlier, you have a choice. Remain in the upset of the news I broke to you a couple of pages ago, or consciously choose to fill your own cup up with your love and self-care, and share from your over-flow.

Take the time to value yourself, to fill your own life with your joy, your successes, your love, your gifts, and you will be more fulfilled by your own self. From this place you can give and receive love in abundance, rather than in lack.

Doesn't that sound a lot healthier and more enjoyable?

And remember - it is your choice.

Notes

Notes

Notes

#2

If you don't respect yourself, your partner won't either. They reflect your self-image. Honor yourself, they will too.

It is amazing how many people are unaware that their romance partner is a perfectly designed mirror for them.

Yes, it is true. We attract partners who will reflect back to us what we are about, either covertly or overtly. This means sometimes it is consciously done, though more often than not, it is unconsciously done. That's how powerful we are, that we can attract that from our partner, even while they (and we) are unaware of it.

And, of course, the inverse is also true. We give that same gift (often unconsciously) to our partners. We provide a mirror to them of their own "stuff" too. This is a good thing, for both partners. Yes, really it is.

This is one of the most profound and powerful learning opportunities you have about relationship. Learn this principle well. It will serve you powerfully and successfully as you move into deeper and more powerful relationships.

In this instance (as in all instances, incidentally), it is important to recognize you have a choice.

If you are feeling that your partner is not respecting you as you wish, before reacting or at least responding to them, consider how you might not be respecting yourself on some level.

Where do you dishonor or disrespect yourself? Ask yourself honestly and clearly. Look through your day, through your life and see if there is something you do or don't do that dishonors the wonderful being you really are.

Do you break your agreements with yourself to exercise, go to the gym, eat more healthily, begin that diet, or get more sleep? Do you forget to take care of yourself in your life?

Do you break agreements in your work life? Do you run late to your appointments? Do you always cut it close to meetings or dates?

It could be subtle or blatant. Whichever it is, it is guaranteed that somewhere in your life you have not been respecting yourself fully. With this reflection, you have been presented with an opportunity to take your self-honoring to a higher level.

The gift your partner presents is to have you take better care of yourself.

And as you improve your own self-care, they will step up more too.

Caveat: it is possible that this person hasn't gotten the message after you stepped up to take better care of yourself, so if they continue to disrespect you, you may consider thanking them, thanking yourself, and leaving for someone who does see you as you now are. There's no call for intentional, continuous abuse, by self or others.

I will go into more detail with this mirror concept in other Chapters, as this particular relationship gift warrants deeper explanation.

Reflect on that.

Notes

Notes

Notes

#3

True romance requires giving your heart, soul & commitment to yourself, as well as your partner. The rewards are priceless.

Society teaches us that it is important to have a commitment to your partner, and to your relationship. This is good.

Actually, this is great.

Commitment is a fundamentally vital part of a deeply passionate, conscious, and monogamous relationship.

What's not spoken of, though, is your commitment to *yourself*, in your relationship.

Consider this for a moment.

Have you committed more to your partner in your past relationships than you did to yourself?

It is OK. You are not alone.

We often put so much emphasis on our relationship partner and neglect our relationship with ourselves when we embrace being in a couple.

I'm sure you've experienced the following scenario:
You meet someone, and you go on a date or three, and you get more and more involved with this other person. You dive in. Then, you get romantic, and then you get it on. At least, that's the intention.

All the while, your commitment to yourself is absent.

This is not unusual, as the romantic doctrine and societal beliefs of the past portrayed co-dependence as a matter of fact. You were expected to be dependent on the other person.

Being self-reliant and self-sufficient was not appreciated, acknowledged or *normal*.

Well, self-sufficiency is a good thing. It is healthy and self-supportive to be self-reliant and self-sufficient.

Being self-supportive, self-sufficient, and self-reliant is necessary for you to have an authentic, powerful, and passionate relationship.

By taking care of yourself and making sure you are the healthiest and best you that you can be, you can be a benefit to your partner as well.

Loving yourself actually attracts more love from your partner, as long as it is a pure intention to care for yourself, not just a means to an end, if you get my meaning?

When you commit to yourself, commit to loving and appreciating yourself, and take great care of yourself, two things will happen.

First, you will have an abundance of love and depth to share with your partner, which they will most definitely appreciate.
Second, your partner will feel free and able to choose each moment to be with you without feeling pressure or obligation, which you will appreciate.

And as a side-benefit, commitment to yourself, to your heart, to your own growth and evolution extends far beyond relationship. It will transform your work, your service, and your family, everything around you.

It is life changing, and yes, it will really transform every area of your life.

You're welcome.

Notes

Notes

Notes

#4

Know your core values. Know what makes you tick. Stay true to your heart, and allow your partner to know you authentically and honestly.

If you don't know who you are, your new romantic partner won't either.

How can someone get to know you, if you don't even know yourself? It seems obvious, yet do you know what makes you tick? Do you know what you value, what is important to you?
Do you know your essential nature?

What is important to you?

What do you believe in?

What do you stand for?

What make your life worthwhile?

50 Ways To Love Your Lover

What do you care about most?

What are you about?

Ask yourself these questions on a regular basis and find out for yourself who it is that lives inside your skin.

As you grow in your self-knowledge and clarity of your core values, you become more authentic, more empowered, and more honest with the world around you. Your self-understanding breeds self-confidence and self-reliance.

Knowing who you are is key to your own integrity and individuality. When you know who you are, you can align to your heart more readily.

Knowing who you are and being aligned with your heart certainly makes your choices in romance much clearer.

Or, to put it another way, declaring your truth internally and externally establishes your place in life, your stance and your dance and makes finding your match so much easier. Is that clearer?

You are a powerful and unique individual and as such have tastes, preferences as well as clear and important core values. You will know what they are, for you.

Do you value depth in romance, rather than playing at the surface level? Do you desire someone who will travel the whole journey with you, or someone who is great for right now?

If you truly want someone who takes responsibility for their own issues and doesn't dump their upsets on you, don't settle for less than that.

Here are some more values for your list that may be important to you: do you require your partner to have kindness to animals, to the level of being a vegan even? Are you committed to your spiritual path, that you want your partner to respect or perhaps participate with you?

What are your core values, your preferences that are important to your identity and uniqueness? Honoring these is vitally important wherever you go in life, not just in romance. However, it is truly game changing in your love-life.

All of this is to say, when you fully participate as yourself, clear, authentic, and self-knowing, you fully participate in love, in romance and in relationship.

Your authentic heart is what your partner can connect to, can respond to, can know about you. Knowing and aligning with your core values is another aspect of being truly authentic.

This is how your partner can truly know you, fully, authentically, passionately, and powerfully.

Enjoy it.

Notes

Notes

Notes

#5

Surrender to your greater possibility in your relationship. Allow your true nature to shine, and prepare to be amazed.

By this point, you realize there are amazing possibilities and levels of intimacy, depth, passion, love, experience, excitement, connection, trust, and more available to you as you grow and become more fully yourself and attract to you a partner who has done the same, and who is fully committed and connected with you.

That's great.

You have done amazing work on yourself, you have taken steps, studied, and learned about yourself, developed a strong sense of self, and know what has stopped you before, and have overcome that. You have healed wounds from your past and made peace with your old relationships.

You are amazing.

Now you have stepped into a new intentional romance.

50 Ways To Love Your Lover

This is a gift.

It is a gift to be in this new romance. It is a blessing to both you and your partner to be together. Be with that recognition.

Surrender to what is possible with this incredible blend of two growing and conscious individuals. Open to your greatest possibility, and be your authentic and powerful self.

Take the time to be present with your partner in your new paradigm, a new way of relating – healthy, intimate, authentic, honest, loving, and more.

Having done your own inner work and transformed your history, releasing your old patterns and beliefs, you will find yourself in your most incredible romance you have ever experienced. Enjoy it all. You have earned this and deserve all the gifts and love you are enjoying.

At the same time, don't slide into complacency. You have learned by now that you are continually evolving and growing, and your partner is also. Be present and aware of how your relationship is evolving day by day, week by week, month by month, and remember to be your best and most real as often and as best you can.

Honestly, most individuals don't live every moment and second remembering all this, so don't beat yourself up if you don't do it every single moment either.

This may feel blunt, however if you've read this far in the book, you are not one to shy away at the first sign of trouble.

Yes, there are times when you will want and perhaps need to check in with yourself, with your partner, and adjust and refine your relationship.

Just like a new car requires regular maintenance and service to ensure it keeps running like a finely tuned machine, so too your relationship will benefit from your regular and honest review and check-in. Consider this principle your preventative maintenance.

Don't take your relationship for granted. Give thanks for the blessings you have. Give thanks for your choices. Give thanks for your partner.

Continue to take care of yourself.

If you notice any old patterns or behaviors showing up, that limit your relationship, or get in the way of you loving more fully, take the necessary actions and steps to resolve and release them so you can even more fully embrace yourself and your romance.

You may well be amazed.

Notes

Notes

Notes

#6

Are you alone, or lonely? There is a difference, and knowing this will remove your blocks to relationship.

If you are single, this particular principle is for you.

However, if you are in relationship, and you feel lonely, there is much more going on. This Chapter will be a good starting point at least.

First, let me clarify the difference between alone and lonely, as they are not the same thing.

Being alone simply means not being with another. It is not good or bad. It is simply what is.

A single person is alone, although they ideally will have a social life and friends, they are not in partnership at the moment. Simple and clear, and no emotional disturbance generated.

Being lonely, however, is an emotional experience that we choose and create. Feeling lonely can make being single an uncomfortable experience, a painful place to be, and can make the choice of being in relationship incomplete, as I'll explain.

Being lonely, while actually in relationship, is indicative of a deeper issue, and a clear sign that you have other concerns, such as choosing your relationship, choosing your partner, loving more fully, or perhaps choosing to leave your relationship. There are many more keys, guidance, and support elsewhere in this book that will help you.

If you are single, and you feel lonely, then you will be tempted to look outside yourself for comfort, for love, for fulfillment. In fact, you will choose relationship as a way to avoid feeling lonely, and to make yourself feel whole.

You will quite likely be thinking "when I get in relationship, I will feel loved, I will feel whole, I will feel so much better."

This is not going to make you feel better. Actually, this is going to be a mistake, and is a path that will be ultimately unfulfilling. Choosing a relationship as a way to stop feeling lonely is actually co-dependence, which I cover in much more detail in a later Chapter.

In simple terms, feeling lonely while single is a clue that you have ignored your own love, comfort, and self-fulfillment, and you feel you are in lack.

If you are in relationship, and feeling lonely, you may have already guessed this is also true for you. And you are putting your need for all that on your partner, which may work, for a short while.

Regardless of your relationship status, you are absolutely enough, just as you are.

In fact, let me remind you.

Make some time to do the following practice. I recommend you take time to do this every day, at the beginning of your day is ideal.

Read the following statements to yourself. One set is written as you talk *about* yourself, the other is written as you talk *as* yourself. You may find one format more potent than the other. Use each or both series as you desire.

Do this in front of a mirror, and out loud, and it will be even more powerful and impactful for you.

Stop for a moment. Take a slow deep breath.

OK, you are ready to begin:

- You are worthy.

- You are divine.

- You are amazing.

- You are sexy!

- You are deserving of the best in life simply because you are here.

- You have enough love to share.

- You are a contributor to the world around you.

- You are important.

50 Ways To Love Your Lover

- You are whole.
- You are complete, right here, right now.
- You are magnificent.
- You are beautiful/handsome just as you are.
- You are so much more than this.
- You fully deserve all you want.

- I am worthy.
- I am divine.
- I am amazing.
- I am sexy!
- I am deserving of the best in life simply because I am here.
- I have enough love to share.
- I am a contributor to the world around me.
- I am important.
- I am whole.

- I am complete, right here, right now.

- I am magnificent.

- I am beautiful/handsome just as I am.

- I am so much more than this.

- I fully deserve all I want.

Repeat as necessary. I did suggest practicing this daily, in front of a mirror, and make it your morning practice before the day gets fully underway. Do this every day, for 30 days, and see how you feel. You may decide to keep going.

Are we clear now?

You don't need a partner to be fulfilled, you don't need to be relationship to be worthy, deserving or complete. In fact, you are all that as you are, and a healthy relationship will simply add to that.

Build and deepen your own self-support, self-worth and self-approval. This may be the most powerful work you do for and on yourself. It will change your whole life, guaranteed.

You will also discover you are more appealing and attractive to a partner, which is a nice side-effect.

Let's review: What is the difference between being lonely and alone?

Lonely, as mentioned, is an inaccurate feeling of emptiness that can only be filled by another. It is one of the core causes of co-dependence.

Alone is being separate from another, it is actually a state of autonomy. Being alone doesn't require anyone else to make you feel OK, and you don't need to be fixed.

I trust this is clear?

Notes

Notes

ABOUT YOUR HISTORY

50 Ways To Love Your Lover

#7

Objects in the mirror may be closer than they appear. This especially pertains to your relationship.

This book is in your hands to help you have more amazing and profound romance, and what you can do to start, manifest (if you are currently single), enjoy and increase the love you have in relationship.

Sometimes, in our lives and especially in relationships, there are upsets and issues that need to be resolved. Being in intimate connection and openness with a partner is a divine crucible where buried hurts, issues and past upsets can be revealed, released, and healed. It is part of the process, so to speak, a benefit and a gift that love provides.

If you want to have the most profound, passionate, and healthy relationship, your relationship skill set must include how to handle upsets with yourself and with your partner, in case they happen (which they never do for you, of course?).

Many times, when (yes, when) you get upset or triggered by an interaction with your partner, you will often feel a resonance with a similar memory that likely pre-dates this relationship. This past memory will overlay your current upset situation with a similar (even duplicate) upset feeling or limiting belief that you judge, or are sad, hurt, or in pain about.

It will be a memory that you probably don't appreciate or like about yourself. This is not fun, yet is worth the steps to resolve and love through.

Keep reading.

For example, you get upset with your partner because they break an agreement with you. Maybe they forgot to pick something up you had asked for and you were upset with them over it, or they said something totally inappropriate that hurt someone's feelings and you reacted.

You might judge your partner as unreliable, or as someone who doesn't keep their agreements. In fact, you realize you have done exactly the same thing. Or you have done (or are doing) even more than they have. You also realize you haven't yet owned up to it. Actually, you haven't yet taken any responsibility for the situation.

As is more often the case, you judge your partner and say something negative about them that you later realize you would say about yourself but haven't owned up to. In fact, you are using them as a scapegoat for judgments that you really feel about a previous relationship, or yourself.

You may notice that your upset feelings far exceed the energy of the situation. This is a clue, a large waving flag in fact.

Check inside and ask yourself if this is something you have done before or said before? Or was it is something that was done or said to you in the past? Your relationship partner is now reflecting back to you like a faithful mirror.

This is perhaps the most challenging and yet rewarding aspect of relationship - the art and science of projection.

This is a view on the mirror of projection that is a blessing even though it may feel like a curse.

One key indicator that this is a projection, as mentioned above is you may have a more reactive upset about what happened, than you would reasonably expect. If so, take note. You are, in fact, projecting onto your partner.

This is an unspoken (and often unconscious) agreement you have with your partner. Your partner will, often times, show you where you have something you can heal, transform and resolve, through the magical art of projections. And yes, you will often provide this gift to your partner too. This is not a one-way street.

Your partner will do this for you almost always unconsciously, not even aware they are doing this. That's the magic of projections, and it does require you to be observant when you get upset. See beyond the surface of any situations that generate reaction in you, get past what may be your initial reactive response and look deeper.

With practice (or with coaching) you will uncover the automatic reactions, disconnecting the automatic reactivity by becoming aware and conscious of the origin of this reactive place, doing the work to heal and release it, and then it will no longer be an automatic reaction.

Once you have resolved the projection, you will be able to see the original real-world situation much more clearly, and deal with it much more reasonably. Your upset and disconnect will diminish and even disappear. Your partner will most likely be very grateful for the fairer treatment too.

50 Ways To Love Your Lover

This is a very cursory explanation and guide to dealing with projections. They are very often buried and less easy to discover or reveal. Becoming aware of the red flags, the warning signs, is a very wise choice, so you will be able to recognize that your upset is misplaced. It will give you a chance to take stock, and ideally resolve this yourself, or better, seek more skilled support and help with this. I do help my clients resolve this once and for all, so their love, their energy and their lives are far more fully expressed.

No, it might not be pretty, or even pleasant. However, it will be a great opportunity to love more, to connect deeper and to become more authentic, both yourself, and with your partner.

Yes, you are worth it.

Notes

Notes

#8

**Your baggage
(aka. your unresolved stuff)
is never caused by your
new relationship.
You attracted your partner
to show you what you haven't
yet resolved. Get to it.**

Baggage? Unresolved stuff? What does this have to do with love, romance, and exciting relationship?

Actually, it has a whole lot to do with your choices and your success, or lack of it, in romance.

Yes, this is important. You may be tempted to skip ahead. This is not the prettiest topic, however this is a key subject where you will have the deepest paradigm shifts in your love-life.

Let's begin by clarifying the term baggage, what it means, as well as what unresolved stuff you might be *carrying*. It will be worth it for you, trust me.

Baggage, relationship baggage in particular (yes, this is contextual to this book), is a collective label for all the emotional upsets, behavioral patterns and limiting beliefs that you have accumulated in your history of romance and life, and which you drag from relationship to relationship.

If you are like most humans, you learned your earliest lessons about love and relationships from the adult role models you had when you were very young, called parents, relatives, etc. Your earliest relationship beliefs are formed at the feet of your adult role models, and usually before you have formulated your own independent conscious beliefs and patterns.

These beliefs and patterns are taken on automatically as the way things are. As you matured, these beliefs and patterns were buried in your subconscious yet they are directing your way of being in relationship.

Then you begin to add to that collection of beliefs, experiences and lessons you have in your relationships, and it becomes a mass of subconscious and automatic programming, aka. baggage.

Yes, you drag all this stuff, like overstuffed suitcases and baggage, from relationship to relationship. For some of you, it might be a diminutive handbag or attaché case. For some of you, however, it is a stack of steamer trunks and wardrobe cases.

You are dragging this lovely designer baggage throughout most of your life in all areas. It impacts your life in all sorts of places and interactions as it influences your behavior, your beliefs and your way of interacting.

If you think avoiding relationships will keep your baggage at bay, it won't work. Your baggage will continue to impact other areas of your life.

It is when you are in a relationship; in fact, you will see your baggage in sharp contrast. It becomes more visible and accessible, which is a good thing. This is actually your best place to unpack and see your baggage clearly so you can take steps to release it once and for all. This is a good thing, if you are ready to stop dragging this stuff around. You are ready, aren't you?

If it is any consolation, you probably didn't know about this before, as this baggage is usually hidden in your subconscious.

We humans generally don't enjoy pain. Given the choice, we prefer pleasure every time. And if we can't get to pleasure, any way to avoid pain is preferable to facing it, so even being numb is preferred to dealing with the pain.

Many people, in fact, will metaphorically bury their heads in the sand or at least stuff the painful memories so they don't have to deal with them, and they won't feel too much pain or hurt. You, of course, don't do this, do you?

This avoidance of pain and desire for pleasure or numbness obviously doesn't solve your baggage problem.

Have you noticed how you seem to *automatically* attract certain partners? By doing so, you perpetuate certain experiences and behaviors. This is simply called serial relationships. There are a couple of ways you attract your serial relationship partners.

One way is to maintain the facade of everything is OK. You will attract someone that makes you feel a little, but doesn't step on your sensitive areas, your baggage. This is rare, and frankly very boring.

There is another way you attract your serial relationship partner, and it is the more common path, and leads you to the opportunity to make a change. You are ready to make the change, as you have already read this far.

Because you have a particular behavior or pattern safely buried in your unconscious, you will almost automatically attract a partner who displays or presents that very pattern or behavior you have hidden away inside. It is like an automatic pilot that unerringly guides you to a partner who will show you where you are not yet healed.

Keep breathing.

And keep reading.

This new relationship will stir a feeling within you that is, in fact, the latch to your heaving bags of upset that you have been dragging behind you for perhaps many relationships. OK, I may have pushed the metaphor a little far, however you get the point, I trust.

This specially selected partner comes bearing a mirror to reflect to you your own unresolved stuff.

Another way this blessing can occur (yes this is a blessing, trust me) is you will attract a partner whose patterns perfectly complement, reflect, correspond, or dovetail with yours.

Rather than mirroring or duplicating the same experience for you, your partner's patterns will interlock with your patterns, just like jigsaw puzzle pieces. It may be easier to illustrate this with an example.

If you have a history of feeling abandoned in relationship, until you have resolved this pattern, you will automatically (yes, *automatically*) attract someone who will not be there for you.

They will have their own pattern that dovetails with yours, such as not feeling comfortable being intimate, so they will avoid being close, and in fact will abandon you in some way, perhaps being consumed by work, and not being physically available much of the time. Or to stay safe themselves, they may be emotionally unavailable which to you will feel like you've been abandoned again.

I trust you understand.

Whether you experience your baggage by reflection or by interaction, you have an opportunity, a gift, and an opportunity to change your paradigm, your patterns, and your history.
This is a good thing.

Now you are aware of these bags, you now have a choice if you wish, to take action with simple (and powerfully healing) steps to resolve these patterns, behaviors or beliefs that your partner has stirred within you.

Relationship baggage can be resolved. In fact, you want to resolve this baggage, for your health and well-being (and relationship success), truly.

Burying or ignoring it may work for the short-term, however it will not work for your heart's health, nor will it benefit your romance or relationships. It will absolutely mess up your partnership choices and love-life again and again, until you do.

You have a choice then. Pretend to ignore your baggage when it surfaces, like you may have done regularly, up and until now, or make a conscious choice to work through and resolve it.

I highly recommend the latter choice, of course.

Yes, resolution, release and freedom from your buried upsets, judgments, and other assorted baggage, are absolutely possible. You can be free of all your old limiting patterns, beliefs, and behaviors (your baggage) once and for all. It will take some effort on your part, though.

Baggage is a messy and usually painful subject, which is why it is often ignored and buried. And to make it weightier, you often leave a relationship carrying some amount of baggage with you, which adds to the load.

That is, unless you are extremely conscious of what you do in your relationship and clean up any emotional and behavioral mess you leave behind. This is the more advanced work, which I do recommend if you are truly dedicated to your most fulfilling relationship.

There are powerful tools and guidance in the upcoming chapters to help you heal your own baggage.

Once you clear out and heal all your past baggage, which is very possible, you have to continue with that in mind. Do your inner work as it shows up, take ownership of your own issues and judgments that show up in your romance, and complete all relationships in love with your partner, and you can walk out from that relationship free of baggage.

That is a very high-level choice to live by, and a very conscious and honorable way of being in relationship.

Baggage not required.

Notes

Notes

Notes

#9

Stop projecting your childhood experience onto your lover. You will be free to love and share as you, authentically & freely.

Childhood experience? We are all influenced by our upbringing from when we were children.

That may seem obvious, however I wanted to make this clear.

Your parents (or the adults who played this role as parents, such as grandparents, stepparents, etc.) taught you all about life, when you were young.

You learned how to behave, how to act, how to talk, and a lot more, most often adopting these lessons automatically, without the intentional education your parents may have planned.
You learn more from how they behaved, more so than simply from what they said.

I mentioned this in the previous chapter; however, it bears repeating at a deeper level. How you are in the world, and ultimately how you experience love and romance, is largely influenced by your upbringing, which mainly means your parents.

You learn about relationship not only from how they interacted with each other, but also how they treated you growing up. This was not just about what your parents said to you or told you how to be. You learned more readily by their actions, by what they did with each other and other adults.

They modeled for you what you believed was a *normal* relationship, whether it was healthy or not. You learned from their examples, for good or bad, for better or worse.

This included learning what you believe to be normal about how relationships look, sound, and feel.

You therefore believed, from your parental example, what love should look, sound, and feel like.

Even if you read romance novels or watched all sorts of TV shows or movies about relationships, you will still have innate subconscious beliefs that were instilled from your parents' model.

For you, the example set by your parents may have been great, and you grew up as a well-adjusted individual and relationship partner. If you were raised and loved unconditionally by your parents, and you learned how to live (and love) from their example, you are likely to have high self-esteem and self-trust, and to be an open and loving person.

Good for you.

On the other hand, and honestly for the majority of us, the example set by your parents was perhaps not perfect.

Their parental input to you maybe lacked some elements of love or caring, or it was convoluted somehow, or their way of communicating loving was hidden, or price-laden, or otherwise filtered, or they were never around, or they had abusive tendencies.

The list goes on, however the ultimate result is you repeat what you learned in your own relationships, the good, the bad, and the ugly.

As you grew up, you were not always successful and confident in romantic relationship. This is often the main cause of a limited or even somewhat dysfunctional experience of loving.

You express and share love in your relationships the same way you learned it from your adult role models. Whichever way you experienced love, it will generally influence how you share love in your own relationships.

For instance, maybe your experience of love from your parents was mingled with control, or withholding, or abandonment, or exchange for something, or abuse of some kind, or neglect. Whatever flavors you experienced, will be limiting on your ability to love clearly and authentically.

Perhaps you were loved in an empowering or encouraging manner. This will influence your ability to love in a positive and uplifting direction.

You will attract partners that perpetrate the same relationship patterns you were raised with, and this will happen without your conscious focus or intention, it is an automatic part of your life, perpetuated by your subconscious mind.

This could be great, or could be scary, depending on your relationship history.

That is the way it is.

Until you make it conscious and make a conscious choice to change it. When you become *consciously* aware of their influence, you can take action to change your way of being in relationship.

You can attract a whole different experience of loving and romance in your relationship when you can look back at your relationship history and see what your patterns and behaviors were, clearly, and with some changes, step out of that paradigm and behavioral pattern.

Of course, that may be easier said, than done.

A great place to start is taking time and focus to review your personal history, particularly in your younger years. Review and witness how your parents did or didn't love each other, how they were with you, how they showed affection and caring, and how they expressed emotion.

All this will show you a lot about how you are, in relationship. You might be very surprised at what you discover.

There are steps to take to release and forgive and be grateful for the past, which I won't go into here. There are many ways of changing your paradigm, which can include therapy, group work, reading transformational books (like this one), or working with a coach such as myself.

Supporting yourself and transforming your past may require the assistance of an experienced guide or counselor. A great choice is someone whose mission is to help you in this area. If you want a paradigm shift, I recommend you seek assistance.

After these important steps, you can make some new choices. If you realize you've been feeling victimized in your relationships, and you recognize that was a paradigm in your parents' relationship, you can make a different choice to be empowered in romance and relationship.

Changing your history and your way of being in relationship is powerful and life-changing work, and will bear fruit and many blessings in your life. It will be forever changed and transformed. You will be free to love as you choose, rather than being entrained to be a certain way that you didn't even realize you were doing.

Once you have faced this and released this past history, your relationship experience will shift dramatically, and your love life will be authentic and magical.

And you will attract a completely different type of partner and lover, as they will no longer mirror or reflect these old patterns.

You will be free to love as yourself, wholly and completely.

Notes

Notes

Notes

#10

It is not your job to forgive your partner.
It is your job to forgive yourself for your own judgments.

This one is a little controversial (none of the other 49 are, of course!).

It is not your job to forgive your partner. In fact, it is not your job to forgive any other person, either.

What?

Keep breathing.

Before I explain this fully, I will illustrate something first to set the stage, so to speak.

Most likely at one time or another, you've gotten upset with another person. Perhaps it was a past lover or romantic partner (they might even have been the same person). Of course, this happened far back in your life history, before you became so mature, advanced, and wise.

You may have felt resentment, or judgment about their way of being or how they talked to you. Perhaps you felt put upon, or ignored, or even abandoned. Or your upset could have been because they didn't keep an agreement, they had made with you.

Most of these triggering feelings usually have a common core feeling: resentment.

In case you didn't know, the effects of resentment on your own psyche and humanity are not good.

This quote might shed some light: "Resentment is like taking poison, and expecting the other person to die."

You think this is a dramatic statement?

Well, yes it is.

However, it also bears truth. It has been documented in scientific research that anger has been linked to heart disease, and judgment (of which resentment is a particularly vehement form) has a negative and toxic impact on your body, literally it is a poison that diminishes your body's ability to function and thrive.

In case you were wondering, if you judge yourself, you are turning that same upset and judgment inward toward yourself, you know this as guilt.

It might feel better to you to resent someone else rather than feeling guilty. Guilt, however, is just as toxic as resentment, and the judgment takes its toll on your health. The negative impact on your own body is the same.

There is some good news mixed in with this - if someone is judging you, it is not toxic to you, it is toxic to them.
That's a small prize, I know.

I certainly don't recommend you going out of your way to warn them that their judgments are poisoning their bodies. They might take it the wrong way.

Before we get too deep into this topic, there are a couple of suggestions if you find yourself being judged:

If the other person judges you, it can be a sign that what you did or said was out of alignment, and you might want to change your behavior to come back into alignment.

Alternatively, it may be their own perception that is generating their upset, which has nothing to do with you. If you adjust to suit them, you will become a slave to their needs, rather than being empowered in your own autonomy, so choose how you respond to other's feedback, whether a judgment or not.

I trust you may have surmised by now that the only judgments you *can* and need to truly forgive are your own.

Whether your judgment is of your own actions (or inactions) or of someone else's actions, words, or inaction, it is your own judgment of yourself or them that is slowly sapping your strength and adding toxicity to your system.

Have I made this clear by now? Good.

What can you do about it?

Quite a lot, actually.

You can definitely reduce and eliminate the toxicity in your system, which will save your life. OK, that was a little dramatic.

The most effective way of counteracting, resolving, and releasing judgment is with forgiveness.

Remember back to the beginning of this chapter, I mentioned that you don't forgive another person. That is because the judgments reside with you. You have the judgments, whether against yourself or another person.

So, you get to forgive yourself for these judgments, regardless of where you pointed them.

The agent of toxicity, so to speak, is/are the judgment(s) you've been holding onto. Your relief, your healing path is to forgive yourself for your judgments of your (or their), behavior.

Basically, you forgive yourself for judging what you did or didn't do, said, or didn't say, etc. Or you forgive yourself for judging the other person for what they did or didn't do, said, or didn't say, etc.

One caveat (well, another one) is this: we are all conscious loving individuals who make mistakes occasionally. I believe we do the best we can, so when we know better, we do better. This is one of the reasons I trust this book is helping you enjoy romance better.

This being so, we don't judge the loving conscious individual (including the one in the mirror). We are actually upset about the erroneous behavior we experienced.

So, judgment is associated with the doing rather than the being. Does that make sense?

Who you are beyond all the personality and stuff is perfect and who the other person is, beyond their personality and stuff, is also perfect. What you may be upset about, and judging, is your or their behavior that may have impacted you negatively.

You have the opportunity to forgive their behavior, or more specifically you can forgive *your judgment* of their behavior. Ultimately, it is an inside job.

A reminder and clarification: Forgiveness does not equate to forgetfulness. If someone abuses you, you don't forgive them and stick around. Instead, remove yourself from that abusive situation, take time to forgive the judgments, resentment, self-recrimination, and guilt that you have internalized. Your heart has been burdened by these and forgiveness helps your heart heal before you jump into a new relationship. You will be whole and healthy, so you can love again, and be free.

Here's one powerful reason you will want to have forgiveness as a go-to tool for your health and wellness (emotional, mental, and physical): If you don't forgive your judgments, you will end up as a victim to the other person's actions.

You will be depleting your own health while the other person may well be oblivious. That doesn't seem particularly smart from where I stand.

How about you?

50 Ways To Love Your Lover

HOW TO:

Some of these chapters speak of healing and resolving of upsets. In this chapter, for your use, is a practical option, a method of resolving and releasing judgments and opening to more love.

This guide can certainly be used in respect to projections, resentment, guilt, and basically any form of judgments.
Keep this handy; consider this your "upset resolution quick-start guide." Note that I have provided a more detailed guide (actually two) for you to download for free at the end of this chapter.

You can use any past experience that you have upset emotions or discomfort about. Choose one that you still have a negative charge on, ideally with a partner or ex-partner, to keep the focus relationship specific.

Recall an upset you had with your current or past romantic partner (this does happen for most people), whether it was about something they did, didn't do, said or didn't say. Notice the upset you had on them and on what they did or said.

You probably felt justified and right (even righteous) in your upset at them. They did something wrong, and you are upset about it. That's normal and correct, right?

Not so fast.

Take a moment to review the situation you had with your partner. Look at it, feel into it, and listen to what you remember being said by each of you. Feel the intensity of what they did, and also feel the intensity of what you did. Feel the reaction, not to relive it, but to get a strong sense of how you experienced it and then can release it. By remembering this way, you have more access to the experience and can enjoy more freedom once you complete this exercise.

This is an opportunity to intentionally heal and release this perhaps painful memory, maybe once and for all. I recommend the following process as it is easy to remember and fairly straightforward, which helps when you are dealing with emotional upsets so you can stay on course. To that end, you will want to take some time with each step. Don't rush yourself through it.

This is a three-step process, and each step requires time to work through, as well as your commitment to yourself, your love and your healing.

You can do this by yourself, as long as you choose to do this in a quiet environment where you feel safe and have privacy. You can seek support from someone skilled in counseling, someone who can facilitate you through this.

In fact, I support my clients with this when they need help, and they have tremendous healing, release of upsets and emotional pain, and they discover more love always appears.

The following process comes from the University of Santa Monica (I have much gratitude to them for this powerful technique):

THREE STEPS:

1. **Judgment:** Bring to mind the judgments that you have about the behaviors and the situation, whether that be broken agreements, inaction or wrong action, arguments, or coarse words that were exchanged, etc. What did you judge about what happened or what was said?

   In this step, you are focusing on the actions and words that you remember, not on the person themselves. The judgments are what you have chosen about what they did, not who they are.

2. **Forgiveness:** After you have become present to the judgments you hold, most of which you probably don't have to dig too deep to find, the next step is to apply forgiveness.

   Review each of the judgments you listed. You now have the opportunity to forgive each judgment, one by one, and to release them. Again, the key here is to forgive the behavior, rather than attempt to forgive the person. This person is not defined by what they do or say.

   This person (just like you) is a whole person who has volition, free will, and a personality that may express in ways you don't agree with. It is these expressions that you are triggered by, the behavior or words.

   This may be a new concept for you to grasp — to separate the person from their behavior — so I recommend you take your time with this chapter.

   It may well be a paradigm shift for you, to see the person separate from their behavior, and free yourself in the process. Yes, this is about you and your freedom. You free yourself from the judgment and the toxins through forgiveness. For example: Joe is an ex-boyfriend of yours (or Jo, ex-girlfriend, depending on your gender and preference in romantic partnership). You have a judgment about Joe, as a liar and a cheat.

Yes, it is harsh, and it may have been your experience. The judgment is about what Joe did — he lied and he cheated. Free yourself by the act of forgiving yourself
for the judgment you have about Joe's lying and cheating. Make sense?

OK, now we get to the mechanics. The format of what you say to yourself is this: I forgive myself for judging Joe as a liar. I forgive myself for believing Joe does not tell the truth. I forgive myself for resenting Joe as a liar. I forgive myself for judging Joe as a cheat.

Notice the format — you are forgiving yourself for the judgment that you placed on the other person or situation, or the belief (whether accurate or inaccurate) that you held. For some, this is a difficult pill to swallow. Each person is whole and complete, although they may do or say things that color your perception of them. It is the things they do that you judge, and therefore the things they do that require forgiveness, if you want to be free. This process is often very emotional and tender. It can be self-facilitated, although you can definitely seek a counselor or guide to help you through this, particularly if it is a more traumatic memory.

3. **Reframe:** After the forgiveness is completed (you will know this as you will feel differently both toward yourself and to the other person), take time
to review this situation (literally re-see what happened without judgment). Did Joe lie intentionally? Did Joe make a

mistake? Did Joe believe what was said as true, etc.? Once you have released the upset and judgment with forgiveness, you can now move into seeing the truth more easily, and even be grateful for what is now true, and love yourself more easily. In the example of Joe cheating, presuming he did actually do that, then it is a fact that can't be changed. The reframe for this is that you have learned from the experience, and will be more vigilant with your future partner, to choose more wisely, for example.

This is one of several different techniques for resolving upsets and judgments. I trust this one will serve you well.

It is a deeply compassionate and powerful journey to support you in forgiving resentments, guilt, judgments, and even what may have felt unforgivable.

Remember, this is about your own freedom, self-support, self-respect, and self-confidence. It actually has nothing to do with the other person, although they may not occupy such a dark place in your consciousness when you are done.

To assist you in this process, I offer two different worksheets for you to use for your own self-forgiveness practice.

One of the forgiveness worksheets expands on the steps shown here. The other is the Radical Forgiveness worksheet taken from Radical Forgiveness by Colin Tipping (more about him in the bibliography at the back of the book).

These are my gifts to you, and all you need do is visit the link and download both forgiveness worksheets at **BarrySelby.com/50WF**.

Feel free to use both and discover which works best for you.

Notes

Notes

Notes

#11

If you love your partner more than yourself, why? If you *use* them to avoid your own "stuff," look in your mirror & grow.

You love your partner? I hope so.

Well, how much do you love them? A lot?

More, in fact, than you love yourself? Do you value your partner more than you value yourself?

Loving your partner is a good thing, in case you're wondering.

Loving yourself as much as you love your partner is a good thing too.

Do you love them so much that your own "stuff" is for all intents and purposes, absent and invisible?

Do you put all your attention on them as a means to ignore, avoid or pretend there is no "stuff" for you to deal with?

In fact, do you love them with all their "stuff" while holding back love from yourself because of your own "stuff"? Does that even make sense to you now?

If you are not resolving and releasing that "stuff" I spoke of earlier, it is quite likely you feel like you love yourself less than you love your partner.

If you love your partner more than you love yourself, you are out of emotional balance. When you put their needs far above your own, and suppress your own needs and self-care, something is off.

If this is true for you, where are you holding back with your own self-love? What are you choosing to believe about yourself?

What rule or belief are you using as a reason to hold back how much you love yourself compared with the love your shower on your partner?

Perhaps it is that "stuff" you have that's unresolved from your past in your own life. If you've been reading this book from the beginning, you will have realized by now that I believe relationships are powerful and rich places to grow and become better at being you. And consequently, you will have "stuff" show up in your relationships – issues, upsets, misunderstandings, disagreements, and arguments, etc.

There is also your internal "stuff" – feeling unworthy, not feeling confident, self-judgment, comparison, not feeling approved of, etc., which is often the source for your external "stuff." By the way, that's a powerful tip, right there.

Your limiting self-talk, your distorted self-image, your emotional upsets, your negative beliefs and their kin can really get in the way of your love-life. They will become blocks in the way of your own heart's expression.

These blocks will actually create a wall between you and your partner. It will make seeing and loving them clearly more difficult. You will see them through the inaccurate lens of your limited perception, and you will internalize this distortion on yourself.

Which will lead to even more "stuff" and upsets to deal with.

Re-read the last couple of paragraphs again. Do you notice this could become a futile (and painful) exercise in insanity (doing the same thing again and again, expecting a different result)?

Authentic and profound romance can only truly be expressed when you love yourself fully. Yes, you can love yourself despite your unresolved issues, and yet, if you don't resolve all that stuff, or at least are in the process of doing so, how much do you really love yourself?

Are you ready to take a different path? Are you willing to take a different path? These are different questions by the way.

Take a good look at what makes you tick, your "stuff." What is your trigger for your avoiding behavior? Be willing and open to facing that trigger, the "stuff" that you have not wanted to face before, and transform it, with help of course! Work with a counselor, a coach, a therapist, or if you have the faculty and skills of your own, self-facilitate your journey to healing and transformation. You will become more whole, more alive, more vital, and your partner more visible and connected to you.

Let your partner love you as you are, even with your "stuff." You do it for them, after all, so let them love you the same way, as you are. Let their love remind you that healing and releasing that old "stuff" is absolutely worthwhile, and you will express more of your love to them.

It is worth it for you to heal and grow beyond your history, and it is absolutely vital to your own self-esteem, self-confidence and self-support. And it will transform your relationships from here on out.

When you cleared out that "stuff" completely and successfully, your heart will be free to love fully and openly, and your life will be a whole lot more full and vital.

How's that for you?

Sounds like a good thing to me.

Notes

Notes

#12

Lovers come and go. You are the constant in your relationships. Do your inner work and become the best you.

You are the common participant in all your relationships (yes, kinda obvious). It makes sense then, that you are the constant in your relationships, and as such you have the gift and ability to change how your relationships are to enjoy and grow in.

You may have noticed this perspective has been expressed a lot elsewhere among the **50 Ways To Love Your Lover**, although it was usually in relation to a specific topic or theme.

Let's face the "elephant in the room," so to speak.

This principle is really one of, if not *the* core principle of all the principles in this book. Kind of "one ring to rule them all" in **Lord of the Rings** parlance, this principle is the root behind many of the other principles you are reading about here.

You are indeed the one constant across all your relationships, in case you never consciously noticed this before. Any and all patterns that continue, that repeat, that seem to show again and again are therefore extremely likely to be related to your presence in the relationship, rather than your ex-partners.

Yes, you can keep dancing from relationship to relationship, hoping or believing that your luck will change, and this relationship will be different from *all* your previous ones. Fact is, without changing yourself, that *ain't gonna* happen.

You are absolutely the center of what's happening in your life and in your world, and that includes your relationships, whether intimate or general.

If you notice that a certain experience, habit, pattern, belief, behavior, or issue shows up again and again, regardless of which relationship, this is a sign. Consider this a wake-up call, a call to action, a call, in fact, to do some homework.

Truth be told, it is up to you. If you are comfortable in a generic and bland relationship, that lacks, power, passion, and pizzazz, keep doing the same old thing, and you'll get the same old result. If you want to have an amazing, incredible, and glorious relationship, do the inner work necessary to be the person you want to be, so you can be the one who can have that.

It is my passion and purpose to assist my clients in transforming their experience, so they attract their dream romance, the relationship they've been dreaming of. Perhaps they've been dreaming about this for a very long time. I suspect it is your desire and dream as well to have amazing love and romance.

It takes courage and commitment to take these steps. It takes willingness and honesty to face your own history, your own patterns, beliefs, and behaviors that have been playing out in past relationships again and again. And it is worth it. The rewards far exceed your effort and work.

Know what you really want, and you can transform yourself and your way of being so your heart will be clear, and then you will attract your heart's desire, powerfully and authentically, and your relationship will be magical and incredible.

It is abundantly clear to me that until you handle your own stuff, you will deny yourself your ultimate relationship. By doing your own inner work, you will in fact become the ultimate you, which will automatically attract your ultimate relationship. You deserve this.

You have a choice.

Choose wisely.

Notes

Notes

Notes

ABOUT YOUR JOURNEY

50 Ways To Love Your Lover

#13

There are many books on romance.
There are trainings too.
Yet, the real education happens
when you are <u>in</u> relationship.
Study well.

I have read many books, studied with many master teachers, participated in many diverse and interesting seminars, workshops and intensives on the theme of relationship, love and what we're about.

I have gained a broad and deep understanding of love, romance, relationship and more.

I've even written a book on romance and relationships (hint: you're holding it), so I believe I know a fair amount about how to create true romance and profound relationship (and also what not to do).

And yet, with all of that available learning, and yes, even with this amazing book you hold in your hand, it is still the actual participation, commitment and experience of relationship that truly opens you up, and you learn the most.

What I mean is simply this: shifting from understanding and theory to actual practice is the true education.

I'm not talking about school or academia here. I literally mean "education." The word education has a Latin root – *"educe"* – which translates to "to draw forth from within."

It is this opportunity to draw forth your own gifts, your own understanding, your own truth, and loving nature more fully than before. This is where your study deepens.

Putting into practice all that you have learned, taking all that theoretical study, and experiential learning and opening yourself up to even deeper understanding, learning and love, that is the mission, should you choose to accept it.

This is where the rubber meets the road, so to speak. I know from my own experience, and yes, listening to my clients that, without making the learning and education real, it has no value.

It is rare enough for someone to focus their efforts on self-improvement, particularly with the specific goal of having healthier and deeper relationships.

And it is even more rare that someone would then incorporate all that they have learned from their studies and trainings and reading into their next relationship.

It takes practice, and more practice, and acceptance of your journey to give yourself a break, and practice some more. This is not the easy road, not by a long shot. It is, however, the most rewarding and fulfilling road though.

You are in the small minority if you are reading this book. Consider yourself one of the lucky few, whose future in relationship is so far beyond the norm that you will be filled to overflowing with love and joy! Yes, the rewards are bountiful and wonderful.

Taking the lessons contained herein and actually applying them, this is your "homework." Take all that you have learned, both in study of the art of romance, and what your own history has offered as teaching for your future romance.

You will be grateful, and they will be thankful.

Are you ready?

Notes

Notes

Notes

#14

Freedom is a primary quality in authentic relationship. Freedom to express, freedom to grow, freedom to love beyond limits & more.

To some individuals, especially someone who didn't choose this book (or any other books, trainings, seminars, or study like it), relationships are often the antithesis of freedom.

To these individuals in particular, relationships are limiting, relationships are separate and away from their regular life, relationships are even at times stifling.

For these individuals, relationship means a lack of freedom, a feeling of being trapped, not feeling able to do what they want, etc. For them, relationship does not mean freedom, nor does it provide them any sense or experience of freedom.

These individuals will only date at the surface level, never truly diving deep into intimacy and relationship with one person. In fact, some will date multiple partners, keeping their heart protected and not exploring any true depth with a partner.

From my perspective, they simply don't know what they are missing.

I hold a different perspective.

Being in a deep, passionate, rich, and embracing love relationship is an incredible opportunity to embrace more freedom and openness, than you ever thought possible.

In truly empowering and authentic relationship, you are free to be yourself. To be more overt, more expressive, and more focused on your relationship and your partner, and beyond to the people and world around you.

Your attention will be outward focused, out of your own head and introvert space, and into the relationship.

Being single is a form of freedom, although it is not necessarily as fulfilling as freedom in authentic relationship. You have the apparent freedom of being alone and unattached.

Or you can embrace intimate and passionate relationship and experience a whole new level of freedom that is so much more profound and expressive of your true nature.

There is freedom to express, to grow, to love and more, when you are single. Yet, the opportunity to express, to grow, to love and more while in relationship is magnified absolutely.

You will discover levels of freedom in your heart that can only be revealed, uncovered and expressed when you are totally intimate in relationship.

This is not about sex, by the way, although that's yet another level of freedom that you can explore only in relationship.

Where was I? Oh yes, freedom in relationship.

The freedom I speak of in relationship is to take down the walls that you may have kept up to protect yourself, to keep others out, to maintain a sense of normalcy and stability, none of which is necessary or wanted in truly intimate and authentic relationship.

Who you become when you are no longer confined within a presentation of yourself, the "perfect" version you portray to the world is totally different. You relax and allow your heart to shine like never before, and your emotional freedom is natural and authentic as well.

When someone first falls in love, they look so filled with love and joy and their light, it tends to be presumed to be euphoria, chemistry, first attraction, etc., yet it is the first blossoming of this suppressed freedom.

The love and joy that is welling up is no longer constrained, it is freely flowing, which can be a continuous experience, not just a passing phase that ends after a few months or weeks.

When you are in relationship, explore how free you can really be, in your heart, in your soul and in your joy.

You may just be surprised.

Notes

Notes

Notes

#15

There is always more to have in romance: more depth, more intimacy, more love, more fun, more connection and more, and more.

Yes, it is true.

Relationships are never closed ended. There is always more available, more to share, more to embrace and more to enjoy.

This is good news if you are ready for truly authentic and deep romance. In fact, if you want and are ready for deeper connection, greater love, more passion and fulfilling relationship, you are in luck – there is *always* more to embrace, to love and to share in romance.

You might have had a wonderful relationship in your past, and think it may never happen again.

It can, and it will. And it can be a lot more fulfilling and amazing than anything you have experienced in your past, in fact.

For each and every one of us – there is always more love to share, more joy and connection to grow and express.

This is very refreshing and exciting news if you have found yourself despondent about having a good relationship or feeling that all the good ones are taken. Truth is, there's always someone great to be with, someone to share with, someone to grow with, and someone to explore life with.

For some that may seem overwhelming, for others it is a blessing and something to keep you excited and enthralled with romance.

I suspect you are firmly in the latter category, as by reading this book, I can tell you have desire for more depth in your love-life, and certainly in your romance and relationship.

How do you embrace more and more and more? Simply, open to it. Yes, simply be open, be receptive, and be willing to grow with your partner.

More intimacy? Be open, and share and receive.

More depth? Be open, and explore and trust.

More connection? Be open, and let your partner in deeper.

More love? Be open, let your heart guide you and let the love in, as well as out! Sometimes we forget it is a two-way process.

Actually, you may realize that these invitations are all interconnected. By continually being open, and yes, opening your heart, you attract deeper and deeper romance. All that you wish for, all that is available is yours.

When your love for the discovery of new aspects of your partner becomes a pleasure and a gift you seek, you have moved from being in love with your partner to loving your partner with a deeper sense of honoring and appreciation, that takes your own love to a much more profound and vibrant level.

You are in loving with your partner, which is a much deeper and profound level of romance.

More and more.

Notes

Notes

Notes

#16

If you choose your partner solely because they look good, you will have a two-dimensional romance. Love in 3D (depth).

Maybe it is an "LA thing" or a Hollywood portrayal, however it seems more common in the past decade or two that relationship attraction is based almost exclusively on looks rather than content.

Glamorous magazines are filled with ads and promotions showing models who are "the perfect specimen" whether a man or a woman. They have beautiful smooth skin that shines in the camera, their hair is perfectly coiffed, their faces a free of any wrinkles or blemishes, and their bodies are in such perfect shape, tone, musculature, and definition, that one wonders how they even have time to get away from the gym to pose for the photographs.

Then there are the movie stars, TV show leading men and women, and more.

We've been influenced, by mass media and marketing, that we must look like the latest and greatest product users to be successful and have what we want, to the extreme. On top of that, is the clothing, the cars, the accessories, the bling, the house and accoutrements, the tech toys, and gadgets, and so much more, that it seems you must have, if you ever hope to get what you want. Of course, this requirement also extends to what our mates *should* look and be like, as well.

With all that incessant and persistent messaging of how everyone should look, isn't it any wonder we believe we should only be attracted to the most physically beautiful person we can find?

When we look for a mate, a partner, or even a date, we have been "trained" or, more accurately, *entrained*, to be attracted to someone who looks good, meaning they fit the criteria we have been inundated with by the media.

And of course, if we ever hope to attract that sort of mate, we must look the part too. The beauty, fitness, and cosmetic surgery businesses would not be as successful as they are, if this was not so.

It is a beautiful illusion. It is a false image. It is an untrue portrayal that, unfortunately, becomes the unattainable "Holy Grail" we believe we should seek.

OK, perhaps this reads more like a rant. I believe we have been slowly but surely programmed to only see beauty through the lens presented by media examples, rather than by what the heart feels. It has happened over decades, in ways we barely noticed. Just look back at advertisements through the years, for example, remember ads promoting cigarettes as the key to make a man look cool, or a woman more independent. Times have changed, the messaging hasn't.

This is your wake-up call to start to see others authentically, as they really are, without comparison to the standards portrayed all over mass media and marketing.

Getting to the core of this principle, the lesson is this: make your choice based on how the other person feels to you. Yes, looks are important, and yet they will evolve and perhaps fade over time. If your only point of attraction to your mate is their face and body, then your attraction will also fade over time, unless much money is spent on surgery, makeup, and other cover-up tools.

Having said all that, we can always treat ourselves with dignity and respect, including how we take care of our bodies, health, skin, etc.

Take care of yourself, treat your body as a temple and respect and nurture it. Being healthy is not only to live a longer and healthier life; it is also an authentic and truly attractive quality to the opposite sex.

One great opportunity to share in relationship is physical activities that you both enjoy, that improve your health and also bring you together.

For the single reader, as mentioned in other of the principles in this book, when you do things in the world that you love, you will often find a great partner, who is of like consciousness.

Physical health and the pursuit of self-care is definitely a worthwhile area in which to invest your time and energy.

Who knows, you could meet your ideal partner while working up a sweat on a hike, bike riding, or participating in team sports, or maybe you'll cross paths with someone special shopping for groceries for your next healthy creation.

Be open to what's possible. Recognize that what attracts you to someone may well be the light that shines from their eyes that you recognize as the health that they exhibit.

50 Ways To Love Your Lover

Wouldn't it be interesting if they were attracted to you similarly?

Now that would be cool.

Notes

Notes

#17

Relationships are like rubber bands. They stretch, they flex and if overly extended, they will break.

Something I find rather obvious is relationships constantly change and evolve. I've definitely noticed, with my clients and with my own journey, how relationships rarely stay static.

This change and evolution, however, is rarely consistent and parallel between partners, at least, not without conscious intention. What do I mean by that?

Simply this. Each partner in the relationship may or may not be learning new things or growing and changing at the same or different times to the other.

One might be studying a new way of living (yoga, exercise, healthier food choices, for example). The other partner, at a different time, may be discovering his or her own power and gifts. Perhaps a new career choice is happening for one.

These different changes and experiences, which are unique to each partner, put tension on the relationship, similar to stretching a rubber or elastic band.

The result is the relationship has been stretched, in one way or another, and the two partners are at opposite edges of the elastic band that contains the relationship. There is a tension present. This is neither good nor bad, it is simply what is so.

This tension cannot ultimately sustain. Something has to give, to yield. There are three routes that can happen to release this tension:

1. The second partner, who didn't explore new things, or grow in their level of understanding of themselves feels the tension between them and the first partner, and finds out what their partner has been learning and joins in. This second partner grows and the tension on the relationship is reduced.

2. The first partner, who has been exploring new vistas and experiences, realizes that they are leaving the second partner behind, and chooses to forgo these new experiences to be comfortable with their partner. The equilibrium in the relationship is restored once again.

3. The first partner continues their forward development, and the second partner stays where they are or chooses a completely different path to follow. The tension on the relationship is too great to sustain the connection - the elastic band breaks - and the relationship ends.

The second example can be viewed as a possible co-dependent scenario, although in some instances the activities and practices the first partner may be pursuing can be detrimental to them and their relationship, so the choice to forgo these practices would be a healthier choice.

The tension mentioned earlier could also be due to a trauma that happened to one partner, such as a car accident or injury, that didn't happen to the other partner.

A trauma-based change would unfold differently, with the following three paths to tension release:

1. The partner who suffered the trauma would benefit immensely by the other partner being connected, loving and supporting them and participating in the healing process so the first partner regains their wholeness once more. This reduces that tension previously mentioned and the relationship actually deepens.

2. The partner who suffered the trauma may do their own healing, separate from their partner. This can work, however it is often a cause for separation between the partners, and ultimately it can be a trigger that actually ends the relationship (the elastic band breaks).

3. The first partner's trauma preoccupies them and they are more focused on that than their partner, the second partner either ignores the first partner's pain and suffering, or avoids it by focusing on something, or someone, else. This is the least ideal example, and certainly not the choice for conscious and aware relationship.

50 Ways To Love Your Lover

Each of these examples is a real world possibility for your relationship and love-life. Being conscious and aware of this can be the act that reduces the tension that can show up, and keeps your romance and relationship in balance.

You are fully able to choose your participation with your partner, and being present to the changes and evolution of your relationship will show you what you can do to deepen and strengthen what you have.

It is your choice.

Notes

Notes

#18

Relationship is a spiritual practice. Treat it with devotion, discipline, responsibility & love, and you will blossom & grow.

Just like meditation, prayer or other spiritual practices, your relationship is a powerful practice to deepen in your loving and open up your heart, your connection to Spirit and your life.

Romantic relationship is something very special in life. It deserves honor and respect, and is worthy of making a primary aspect of your life. If you choose this, you will grow and deepen in your own expression of love, of joy and of understanding of yourself and others.

It is not just a convenient place to hang out.

Treating your relationship, and by the same token, your partner and yourself with devotional love, and being responsible to make your relationship a priority in your life will benefit each of you and the relationship itself.

50 Ways To Love Your Lover

Romantic relationship is an honoring practice, an opportunity to connect more deeply with another than perhaps you have ever experienced before. By honoring yourself, your partner, and your relationship, you will be filled with a deeper connection to your Spirit, soul, God, or whatever label you use.

For some individuals, it is safer to love at the surface level, to avoid any depth, intimacy, honoring of the other etc. That's not what this book, and I trust, your romance intentions, are about.

Do you prefer to love on the surface, spreading your love more widely, or do you prefer to dive into the depths of love, to love intimately, authentically, and powerfully?

It really is that simple. You can choose to stay safe, to stay comfortable, and remain shallow in your relationships, loving one person then moving on to another, and another, like a butterfly, staying safe and yes, shallow.

Or you can choose to love and honor and cherish authentically one person deeply, beyond your past experience, more deeply than you even realize or have been before.

Truthfully, loving this deeply is a rich and bountiful spiritual practice, it is beyond any thought, and will surprise you! And it is a sacred act, a devotional act, a dedication to something far greater than yourself, or your partner. It is truly a life-changing spiritual practice.

So how do you begin?

There are many ways of making your romantic relationship a spiritual practice. Here are a couple of ideas to get you started. The rest is up to you.

As a simple and accessible starting point, take time each day, whether at the beginning of the day, or at the end, and list what you are grateful for in your relationship, what you are grateful for about your role in your relationship, and what you are grateful for about your partner.

List at least 10 qualities, experiences, or feelings for each. Make this a daily practice, and you will discover a profound deepening to your relationship.

Another way is to be a witness for your partner. Leave your own agenda and choices out of the picture. Whatever your partner is sharing or doing, be an unconditional witness to them, unconditionally loving to them and their focus.

This does not have to be a 24-hour a day practice, unless you want to, of course. Doing this will bring a new level of support and intimacy forward, and will probably be a very different experience than you have had before.

Can you maintain these simple practices every day for a month?

For three months?

For the rest of your life?

Yes, these practices may require some effort initially, so they may not feel very easy, perhaps. It is not about being easy; it is about being willing to dive deeper than you have before.

It is not required that you do this every day forever, however doing this for at least a month will create a habit that will endure, and you will maintain in consciousness an appreciation for your relationship.

And yes, amazing things will happen, not least of which, your love-life will be more fulfilling than you ever thought possible.

There are many other ways of practicing sacred relationship with your partner. Get creative and try out some of your own invention and inspiration.

I have more suggestions and invitations that I share with my private clients and audiences, which of course, they appreciate.

Are you ready to go deep?

Notes

Notes

ABOUT YOUR PARTNER

50 Ways To Love Your Lover

#19

Never presume you know everything about your partner. You don't.

Think about that for a moment.

Never presume you know *everything* about your partner.

Have you felt that you knew your partner so well, you didn't even need to have them say anything, you knew what they were going to say? And were you right 100% of the time? I suspect not.

How often have you dismissed someone's viewpoint from a place of assumption that you already know everything about them?

This is especially risky in your intimate relationship. Once you've spent time with your partner, it is tempting to think you know all about them.

Don't make that mistake.

We are all amazingly complex and rich individuals, with so much life history, learning, beliefs, and understandings.

Anyone, and everyone, you meet is that amazing too.

And so is your partner. Absolutely. Your romance partner is also that complex and rich in their experience and being.

Your partner is an exquisite manifestation of the divine, and worthy of your exploration and understanding. And in case you didn't catch it earlier, you are also an amazing and exquisite manifestation of the divine for your partner to explore and understand.

What lovely mirrors you both are.

This is one of the best gifts you can receive from your partner, and certainly one of the best you can *give* to your partner.

Choose into your relationship from this perspective. You will honor your partner beyond measure, and they will blossom and open like a beautiful rare flower (or for the men, they will open their hearts and grow in stature and power). Of course, sharing this will encourage the same from your partner.

If you use the excuse that you are bored with your partner to leave your relationship, you are lying to yourself. If you feel that way, look inside and see what the real reason might be. What are you doing to bore yourself? It is highly likely you are using that as an excuse and there's something else going on.

What is real is likely to be one of two truths: Either you are projecting your boredom on your partner (I'll talk more about projections in another Chapter), or, as is quite often the case, you have not committed to the deepest connection between you and your partner.

If you are not willing to go deeper, to invest your love and energy and knowing your partner on all levels, leave so they can be with someone who is willing. If, however, you truly know yourself to be willing to have it all, it is a choice point from which you can recommit and choose to take this relationship even deeper. No more lying to yourself.

It takes true honesty to choose in or out of romance.

Are you willing to go that deep, and deeper?

I thought so.

Notes

Notes

Notes

#20

**With your lover,
see who can give more
to the other,
always from your overflow.
Watch blessings unfold
and love deepen.**

Are you giving so you can get something back?

Are you giving out of duty?

Are you giving to prove something?

Perhaps you give to feel better?

Maybe you give too much and exhaust your own resources?

None of these support you.

So, stop doing them.

I've written elsewhere about being self-supportive and to give to your partner from your overflow. This removes the trap of co-dependence and allows a much more authentic and richer relationship. Let's take this to a higher, deeper, more powerful level.

How can you give more than you currently do to your partner that is absolutely from your abundant overflow?

What can you give more than you currently do to your partner that is absolutely from your abundant overflow?

Noticing a theme here?

My message is simple – love yourself fully first, caring and nurturing who you are, truly and authentically, and then you can love your partner from that abundance and overflow. When you are doing this naturally, then explore the possibilities with your partner who has done the same thing (hint, hint) so you are both in balance and able to give easily. You won't feel drained, tired or used from the experience.

Explore this place of giving, let your heart lead, and share with your partner. And invite your partner to do the same with you.

Now turn up the juice. Give more. Go beyond what's easy and perhaps a little lazy. Make an effort, stretch into something more true, more authentic and more enjoyable, for both of you.

Oh, by the way, you may discover you are also being required to receive more. Ah, this is another level of stretching, which is good for your heart and your health.

Keep giving and receiving like this with your partner, exploring new depths and heights of sharing love and notice how your relationship with your partner, and also your relationship with yourself, deepens, grows and transforms.

You may be amazed and touched by the love and depth that you express with each other, and how that transforms your experience of life, and those around you.

This is a gift that keeps on giving, and the fun part is, there's always more.

Keep on, keeping on.

Notes

Notes

Notes

#21

Listen to your partner, hear what they are truly saying. This will require you to speak less. Not a bad thing.

Some people, maybe even someone you know, tend to like the sound of their own voice.

And they must make sure they tell you how much they know, how great they are, how many people they know, and who they know that's important, special, or famous.

This is often so they can feel validated and noticed.

You don't do that, do you?

Of course not.

Maybe it was the other way around. In the past did you notice yourself doing all the talking? Of course, you don't do that now, do you? Did you find that your partner wasn't opening up to you as much as you would have liked? They clam up and don't share anything. So you had to do all the talking.

Did you really hear what they were saying?

Listen to your partner.

Don't just hear what they are saying. Listen to them.

Go deeper. Listen to where they are coming from.

Go deeper still. Listen to what their heart is whispering behind the words they are saying.

For you this may be a shift in emphasis and even a paradigm shift in your communication.

Yes, this is a refined skill, and will require your intentional focus, connection, and openness to receive what your partner is saying.

It will require you dropping any agenda, positioning, or ego trip.

Besides increasing and deepening your connection and intimacy with your lover (which does not *only* mean sex, for those who need reminding), this approach will open you up to a whole new understanding and yes, intimacy and connection with your own heart and feelings too.

Your relationship will open up to a much deeper connection, a more intimate understanding and profoundly loving connection that will be beyond anything previous experienced by either one of you. And yes, as a bonus, your sexual interaction likely will be richer, enjoyable and satisfying too.

This ability to truly listen to your partner, to hear beyond the surface words, and to hear their soul is something you can practice and allow more and more. You will be amazed and opened up by the power of this level of listening and hearing of your partner.

And a couple of additional bonuses, you will see the world with new eyes, and you will discover a deeper level of calm within yourself as a byproduct.

All that, from truly listening to your partner.

Nice.

Notes

Notes

Notes

#22

Want something from your partner? Give it to them first. It will shift you out of any urge for neediness, and they may reciprocate.

Why do we expect our lover to be telepathic? It seems to be an unspoken law that if you really love each other, you should automatically know what each other wants.

For example:

You wanted something from your partner. And you waited and waited and they didn't do what you wanted. You spent hours, days or even weeks waiting for your partner to do or give you something, and they didn't deliver. They didn't get your message apparently.

Maybe you wanted your partner to give you a massage, but they didn't even notice or lift a finger to ease your tension. Even after you stretched extravagantly and made subtle and suitable noises to get their attention (you know the ones), they were still unaware of your need.

Of course, coming right out and asking for a massage is completely un-cool and out of the question (isn't it?). Your partner should *know* you are in need of massage, especially if they really *loved* you, because they *must* be telepathic.

Yes, that self-talk was very convincing. Well, maybe not the thoughts about them being telepathic. That would be too obviously crazy.

Yet, if you look back honestly, you will most probably realize you were attempting to use your romance telepathy to get your partner to do something for you without coming out and asking them directly, and it didn't work.

I think you get the point. You do, don't you?

So, what do you do instead?

You could ask, or you could do something unusual - you could give it away. Yes, give it away.

For example, if you want a massage from your partner, and they haven't gotten your subtle hints, give it to your partner instead.

You will be more focused on them, which is a good thing. In your giving, if you are in a healthy and balanced relationship, you will create a state change that will quite likely inspire your partner to reciprocate in some form.

You will also create a deeper connection, and more openness for conversation, which may well lead to what you wanted in the first place.

You are much more likely to get what you want with a direct request, and you certainly stack the deck more in your favor if you already gave your partner what you wanted.

If their response is not the massage you wanted, you can politely redirect them to your need, if needed of course.
Yes, it is OK to ask.

This is an interesting experiment to explore, and the rewards and payoff can be amazing.

Now, if your partner doesn't serve you or act caring toward you even when you ask, perhaps you are not in the relationship that you really want. In fact, this could be a deal-breaker (and yes, I cover that discussion in another chapter in more detail).

This is a shift from the old co-dependent paradigm you may have inhabited into a healthier and more authentic inter-dependent framework.

Much better.

Notes

Notes

Notes

#23

Cherish, worship, honor and respect your partner. If you won't, you simply do not deserve them. And vice versa.

Being in relationship means many things to many people. For some, it is to have someone close, someone warm to sleep next to, and for others, it is someone to talk to, or simply a convenient person to be with.

On the other extreme, relationship can be about the highest possible union of two individuals.

Of course, there are many variations in between these rather general extremes.

This particular principle speaks more to the second extreme. In case you hadn't noticed, almost all the chapters and principles in this book are devoted to you having more of the latter perspective.

If you are reading this book and agree with the precepts written here, then you are more than likely to want the best relationship ever. You want to be the best partner you can be, and to attract your ideal mate.

You also realize (and probably already knew) that it doesn't end there. Attracting your perfect partner is wonderful, and then the work that is required of you to enjoy and deepen in your amazing relationship is spoken of all through this book.

You also know then, that you have a role in this relationship that includes many things, which include what is spoken of here.

You deserve the best, as does your partner. Cherish them, even worship them, honor, and respect them. And allow all that in return, which may be harder for some.

You may have held back in the past, and as a result your relationship likely was not all it could have been, for you or your partner.

You may not have felt worthy and deserving of powerful and life changing romance and passionate relationship. In case you haven't heard it yet, or skipped a certain earlier chapter, you are indeed worthy. You are fully deserving of your incredible romance and relationship.

As mentioned previously, honor and respect your partner. Worship and cherish them. Worship their essential nature, their heart, and their authentic core. Cherish and support their dreams and goals, honor and respect their truth and being.

Of course, you are absolutely deserving to invite them to do the same for you, to cherish and support your dreams and heartfelt desires, to honor and respect your truth and authentic nature, and to worship your true self, your authentic self. You may want to encourage them to read this book, in fact.

This, then, is a sacred choice, and it is most certainly a choice. It will speak volumes about your character and depth as a relationship partner, and also of the partner you will attract.

You only deserve as good as you get, and nowhere is this truer, than how it is reflected in romantic relationship.

Take this truth to heart – if you want the best, give the best, and choose to receive the best.

Honor and cherish your partner, worship them fully and you will have an amazing relationship. One that exceeds any past relationship you have participated in before. It is time to receive and enjoy a relationship that reflects who you really are and the love you truly deserve.

Start now.

Notes

Notes

Notes

#24

Be your partner's biggest cheerleader, support them to manifest and share their gifts and service in the world.

Were you ever a cheerleader? Have you ever played on a team that was supported by cheerleaders? If you have, you know how this feels, how uplifted you can become, how inspiring it can be, and how much better you played.

Being from England, this was not something I directly experienced; however, we did have support from fans and coaches in our sporting events.

So how does this relate to your relationship?

Let me explain the relevance of this for your romance.

When you are in a committed and loving relationship, you are invested in your partner.

Sit with that statement for a minute:

50 Ways To Love Your Lover

You are *invested* in your partner.

I hope you are in your relationship not just to *get* something for yourself. I trust you are there for more than just convenience and comfort.

What I am getting to is this — if you are committed to a healthy, deep and growing relationship, you are in it to give as well as receive. You give support, above and beyond simply loving your partner, or providing for them.

You support them, you support their goals, you support their passion, and you support their dreams. And they are with you to do the same for you.

You make a difference in your partner's life whether you knew it or not. Now you know it.

It helps them (and you) if you know what is important to them. What are they up to out in the world? What are their hopes and dreams? Being a confidant in their heart-felt dreams is one of the most wonderful privileges of being in an intimate and authentic relationship.

Having a teammate in life, in our vision and purpose in life, not just in romance, is incredibly reassuring, comforting, profound and inspiring.

Be that true inspiring support for your partner. Be the most loving and encouraging teammate, and be their cheerleader, and they will thrive as will their heart-felt dreams.

Also be their sounding board, their resource, and their support. Even if all you can actually do (or all that they let you do) is hold their hand when they make that important call, or make them tea when they are busy writing, it is a gift you provide and so appreciated to know you support them.

How many different ways can you support your partner? How fully do you believe in them? Maybe you can believe in them, and their dreams more than you already do?

Believe in their dreams, their vision, and their gifts so they are totally inspired to share their heart in the world. Wouldn't you want the same? Hint: your answer should be *"yes."*

With your love, they will more easily share their gifts in the world for all to benefit from.

Keep remembering that you are together for many reasons, one of which is to share both your gifts and mission in the world, and you are each other's confidant, coach, partner, teammate, and cheerleader.

Until you have done this, you have no idea how incredible elating, inspiring and supportive this feeling and experience truly is. It will absolutely change your life and your relationship, and this action will inspire great work and creativity in you, and your partner.

Do this. It is a gift beyond your experience, and it is a lot of fun.

Notes

Notes

Notes

ABOUT AUTHENTICITY & COMMUNICATION

50 Ways To Love Your Lover

#25

Learn the difference between co-dependence and inter-dependence. Hint: authentic relationship is the latter.

There are many ways to be in relationship, and all of them are workable to some degree or another. Doesn't that sound romantic?

In the context of this principle, there are three main ways individuals participate and interact in relationship that have different levels of success and emotional health for the participants. There is the co-dependent relationship, the independent relationship, and the inter-dependent relationship. What's the difference? And how do you choose one or the other?

Let's investigate, shall we?

Co-dependence is defined as *"of or pertaining to a relationship in which one person is physically or psychologically addicted, as to alcohol or gambling, and the other person is psychologically dependent on the first in an unhealthy way."*

50 Ways To Love Your Lover

This is how many people *did* relationships in previous generations, and frankly this form of relationship is still rather prevalent. People were brought up with the belief that they needed to find someone who made them feel whole. They were looking for their other half, their better half, the one who will make them complete.

Do you notice a theme here? If you are still unsure, listen to any love song from the 70's and 80's, every single one is likely to be a co-dependent love song. Yes, it was that common. It was the only way to be in relationship, it seemed.

Indicators of co-dependent behavior in your romantic relationships include:

- You can't live without them.

- You will never find anyone like them again.

- You can't trust your partner out of your sight.

- Trying to change or fix your partner.

- Looking for approval from them by what you do, rather than doing it because you want to

- Not feeling worthy of them loving you, and biggest of all,

- Putting your partner's needs far beyond and above your own, and not caring about yourself.

Do you really want an addictive dependent unhealthy relationship?

I think not. Cross co-dependence off your list.

For many, the only other choice appears to be independence. Either be single, unavailable for relationship and be totally independent, or be partly in a relationship, where the only thing shared is the bed.

All finances, efforts, and even date-nights are negotiated.
Not very sexy, I know.

Independence is defined as *"not requiring or relying on something else: not contingent: not looking to others for one's opinions or for guidance in conduct: not bound by or committed to another."*

Indicators of independence in relationship include:

- You keep a lot of who you are, your feelings and beliefs, to yourself, and don't share them with your partner.

- You don't trust or share items of value, including finances with your partner, even after marriage.

- You make decisions without regard for your partner, you don't discuss big decisions with each other.

- You keep walls between you and your partner, after all you don't want to lose your autonomy, or fall into co-dependency.

- You only make agreements out of necessity rather than joy and excitement.

- You don't really appreciate or care for your partner's emotions, as that would impact your ability to remain separate and independent.

Yet, it has been the way many relationships "worked" over the years, so people thought it the only alternative to avoid the co-dependent trap. Either that or remain single, which is independence to the extreme.

Hmmm, that's not a very appetizing choice either. Cross independence off your list.

For the wise, there is a third option, and the one I heartily recommend.

Instead of co-dependence or independence, you will have the most delicious and enjoyable relationship when you enjoy one that is interdependence.

What is interdependence then?

Interdependence is described as *"Participants may be emotionally, economically, ecologically and/or morally reliant on and responsible to each other. An interdependent relationship can arise between two or more cooperative autonomous participants."*

Rather than independence, in which the individuals are completely separate and disconnected, interdependence is very much about connection. Rather than co-dependence though, where both partners are completely enmeshed emotionally and unable to separate (it can feel like they are Siamese twins, joined at the hip), you will be able to connect and yet be fully yourself, fully embracing your authentic nature and share with your partner easily and comfortably.

In the context of relationship, interdependence is the ability to interact and connect to another while remaining self-sufficient and autonomous. It is realizing that some things are yours to own in the relationship, and some are your partner's to own. It reduces the temptation of co-dependence, being in need of your partner, and desolate without them.

You can be reliant on your partner, desire them fully, and also not need them so you can function or breathe.

It also provides much needed space to have ownership in the relationship, and to share from your overflow and fulfillment.

And you also have the joy of deep connection and intertwining of energy and life, without a focus on keeping everything separate, apart and all neat and tidy.

If you seek a healthy and authentic relationship that is fulfilling, intimately connected, passionate and rich, there is ultimately only one truly effective way of relating, and that is interdependence.

If you want authentic relationship, one that opens you up, enriches your life, and grows your own love, get to know what interdependence does for your love-life, and share the gift.

It is truly the best way of *doing* relationship.

Notes

Notes

Notes

#26

Telepathy rarely works. Open and honest spoken communication, with love, always works.

It used to be a romantic construct that if you loved someone, you'd know what he or she wanted, without him or her having to say anything about it to you.

How many times have you hoped your partner would know what you were thinking? How many times have you hoped your partner would do something for you that you wanted, without you having to ask them?

Maybe they would tune in telepathically (actually your mental chatter), and they would understand your need without you having to go to the effort of actually saying something to them.

Maybe you resorted to sounds and sighs and other *subtle* indicators to influence them, so you would get what you wanted. And if they didn't *get it* or act accordingly, you would end up resenting them. And they would be oblivious to what happened, and wonder what they did wrong. Of course, this never happened in your relationships, did it?

How would you feel if your partner didn't say a word to you, expecting you to know what they want automatically, and if they didn't get it, they would be upset? Did that ever happen to you?

Not much fun, is it?

Presuming you know your partner is very limiting.

There is a famous saying in businesses that are successful – there are no dumb questions, just dumb assumptions.

This definitely applies to the business of relationship.

Let's get real here.

It is time to drop this old-fashioned and erroneous relationship pretense. Or to put it simply — stop acting crazy. Really.

The core messages here are simply this:

Don't make assumptions about your partner.

Don't expect your partner to know what you want.

Don't expect your partner to know how you want it.

Or perhaps it should read: Don't require your partner to know what you want. Some people have stepped in that trap before.

In addition to creating unconscious tension between you and your partner, it perpetuates a lazy attitude and a lack of investment in knowing your partner. Don't do it.

Be vulnerable, be real, ask your partner what pleases them, ask them how you can assist and support them. And be honest about what you want too.

Be open, be honest, and be real.

Invest your heart, and your caring, in your relationship. Take time to learn about your partner, finding out what they want, and also finding out what they don't like or want.

Taking time to find out about your partner, their needs and their wants, is an investment of the best kind! And it is a demonstration of caring that is real and appreciated.

And of course, be willing to share with your partner what pleases you, even if they don't ask, be willing to tell them (be appropriate please), so they can match you in knowing what works and what doesn't.

One more time – telepathy is not a reliable relationship tool. Asking honestly and authentically is a reliable relationship tool.

Clear?

Notes

Notes

Notes

#27

Failure in communication includes assuming, and saying "I'm fine." State truth vulnerably, share authentically & listen.

Let's talk about feelings, shall we?

It is important to take ownership of your feelings.

It is also important (in fact it is relationship-saving) to stop blaming your partner. Not particularly surprising, I trust.

Even better (and subtler) is to eliminate any *desire* to blame too.

In this chapter, we're taking a step beyond the previous principle. I'm inviting you to get honest and open with your own emotions. This is a deeper layer and opportunity for authentic and vulnerable connection in relationship.

Your partner asks you "How are you?"

Your response is "I'm fine."

50 Ways To Love Your Lover

They ask you, "How are you feeling?"

And you respond, "I'm fine."

They ask you, "What do you want to do tonight?"

You respond, "Whatever you want, I'm fine."

How often, in the past, did your partner, lover, spouse ask you how you felt, and your response was an automatic "I'm fine."?

Or, if they asked you what you thought of something, or what you wanted of them, was your response "Whatever."?

This may appear trite; however it is a common trap couples get into as they continue in relationship, They get comfortable and engage "auto-pilot" with automatic and generic responses to questions from their partner.

It is just as sabotaging to your relationship as blaming your partner.

And it is a lie to your partner, and to yourself.

If you honestly want a deeper and more connected love-life and romance, if you want authentic connection and trust with your partner, speak your truth.

Speak honestly, and own what you say so your partner will see and hear you. Really see and hear you.

Your partner asks you "How are you?"

Your response is...how you are feeling. If you don't know (for some reason), say you don't know, and be open to a deeper response.

This is being honest and real.

Your partner asks you "Where do you want to go tonight?"

You respond with a real choice, even if it is not the perfect one, be honest with what is so in the moment.

Yes, this may be a little odd or uncomfortable initially, yet the results will both surprise you, and also please you, as well as your partner.

Choosing to be this open and real with your partner invites them to do the same with you (no need to wait for your partner to initiate). When they do, and speak from their honesty and truth, do them the service and respect of listening openly, without judgments or assumptions.

This, in case you didn't know, is what intimacy feels like. It is not just about sex, it is about connection, which is a whole other topic.

Be willing to be surprised and blessed by what they say.

They can do the same for you.

This will transform your relationship communication and your romance from ho-hum to amazing and continue the deepening and connection.

If you're ready for this deeper intimacy connection, then implement this, and other, principles in this book and witness your love-life absolutely transform overnight.

Well, it might take a few days, however you can change all the old habits illustrated here completely if you keep this up for 30 days.

Are you ready?

Notes

Notes

#28

He said, she said is pointless,
no one wins.
I feel, you feel, we feel,
you both win.
Remember who you are,
and why you love.

How do you resolve problems and discords in your relationships?

Have you matured beyond yelling at each other and competing for the title of who's right?

Do you still choose sides, and have arguments about who's right and who's wrong? Or to put it another way...

Do you feel you need to convince your partner that they are wrong, and you are right?

Is being right more important to you, than being loving and happy? Really, do you prefer being right?

How's that working for you?

50 Ways To Love Your Lover

Do you wish there was a better way of communicating, particularly when it comes to disagreements and upsets with your partner?

I have good news - there is a better way.

Before I reveal the solution, I have a suggestion for you.
My suggestion – drop it.

Choose happiness over righteousness. Choose loving over being right. Let it go.

OK, now I've got that out of my system, here is the healthiest way to get results that work for both of you: Own your own feelings and perceptions.

That's it. Really.

When you feel upset with your partner, or you feel your partner is upset, share what you feel, starting with "I feel…" rather than "You did…" or "You didn't…" etc.

This apparently simple language change produces two main results.

First, you will automatically take ownership of how you feel and speak from your own trigger moment, which gives you a chance to heal it.

Second, you obviate your urge to automatically jump to blaming and dumping that you may have done before.

When both you and your partner have this freedom, and ownership of feelings on both sides, you can easily be honest and responsive to each other. This choice can change everything in your relationship.

When you take ownership of your emotions, you will remember who you are. You can make a different choice and stop disowning your emotions and upsets. And you can also release any desire to judge or blame your partner. Your focus and sharing will be focused on yourself and from your own feelings.

This choice works outside of your romantic relationships as well. You can find a whole new level of authority and calmness in your business life, your social life, etc. you will empower and transform your entire life.

That's an all-round good thing.

Notes

Notes

Notes

#29

Being honest changes moment to moment, as our perspective changes. Remember that when you talk to your partner.

"The only constant is change" according to Heraclitus.

Change is constant and ongoing.

Change is happening everywhere, just look around.

And this is no different than in our relationships and our lives. We are evolving and changing, constantly, every moment.

Look back over your life. Do you view your life, your world, and your relationships differently now than you did ten years ago, twenty years ago or even twenty minutes ago?

Your views and your opinions are constantly evolving and changing. You are growing and evolving every moment of every day, even if it might appear from time to time that you are not moving an inch.

Recognizing that this is happening may come as a relief to you. It may also be disconcerting if you always feel you are unchanging, or to find out you may not be fully in control of everything that happens in your life.

You are constantly evolving and growing, whether you want to or not. Obviously, you are evolving physically, whether you label it as getting healthier, growing up, growing older, maturing, or some other label.

Knowing this, you understand that your perspective and your point of view is shifting and changing all the time too. And of course, so is everyone else's perspective and point of view.

Consequently, our perspective on truth shifts as well. If we have a paradigm shift in our consciousness from an event or educational experience, for example, your version of truth may have shifted from what it was before the event happened.

Being authentic in your relationship requires that you align and stand in what's real and true for you, even as that truth shifts and evolves.

Truth and honesty are not the same thing, by the way. Truth is, in this context, what is aligned for you, what is simply the facts you believe and what is so. Honesty is being aligned with that truth.

What this means is, though your truth may and likely does change at different points in your life, your honesty can be constant and consistent in relation to your truth, even though your truth is evolving and shifting. You can be honest always, being authentic to the truth that you understand in that moment. Your honesty keeps you connected to your truth.

As a very simple (and obvious) example, my truth (at a much younger age) was that I lived in England, and I thought my life was focused on being a computer programmer. That was my big picture vision back then. I was honest about that, and it was certainly on my curriculum vitae (that's résumé for my American readers).

At the time of writing this book, I live in California and my life and work is focused on serving and educating many people on living powerful and authentic lives of purpose, joy and amazing relationships.

Both experiences are true, yet depending on when you asked me what my life was about, my answer would be different, yet honest. Simply, what is truth changes, and that change is constant.

In your life too, change happens, your truth has shifted and of course, so has your partner's. Don't expect someone's truth to be static or immutable. It will change, almost guaranteed.

The key is that being honest requires no defense, nor does it make you right or wrong. And this is powerful to be free of any need to be right or to defend your position. You will be less stressed, more aligned and a lot happier too.

Caveat: be gentle with others. Sharing your honesty and voicing it is a powerful and freeing way of relating. It can be abrasive to others who are not ready or used to it. Don't be tempted to be righteous, rather be supportive with your words.

It is not about being right; it is about being present and authentic. Be willing to let go of being right. In fact, be willing to be vulnerable.

It is more vulnerable for example, if you realize the position you held is not correct, but you have been maintaining it to save face (which is an unhealthy choice), and you own up to it. Let go of the pretense and show your partner your truth, by being honest, being true with what is, in the moment.

Be honest in the moment, and invite honesty from others, particularly your partner. Understanding this will keep you sane.

Honesty truly is the best policy.

Notes

Notes

#30

If you blame your partner, you will lose.
If you blame yourself, you will lose.
Be authentic and honest, you won't lose.

You don't blame your partner for anything, or yourself at all.

Of course, you don't do this, do you?

Well, maybe not quite.

If (OK, when) you find yourself at odds with your partner, or you feel you are in discord with them, or feeling they have done something wrong, do you find yourself falling into blame?

Do you feel you are right, and they are wrong? Or maybe it is the other way around and you feel they are right, and you are wrong?

Maybe you get caught up defending yourself so you feel OK, and dumping blame on your partner so you can maintain your position of being right?

50 Ways To Love Your Lover

Do you understand this leads nowhere?

You have a choice with the desire to be right. You can be right, or you can be happy. You can be right, or you can be loving instead. You can be right and lose out on what you really want.

All this leads to that old party favorite – the blame game. How many times have you played that game? You may in fact notice that EVERY time you play, you lose. Even if it appears that you win, you notice later, truth is, you lost.

I hope it is clear that blame is not a winning strategy for anyone. In fact, it is a sure-fire way for *everyone* to lose. Blaming separates you and your partner, and you both lose out on the love that you truly want to share.

Yet many of us still practice blame like it is the right thing to do. Let me be clear – it *never* works. Need I repeat that?

Blame is not a winning strategy. As the chapter heading suggests, honesty and authenticity are the winning choices.

By being honest, you have no need to defend yourself; you have no need to remember what was said. You have an expanded and open playing field to engage your partner and the world.

When you choose honesty and authenticity, one of two things can happen. Either you or your partner will open up more than ever before, and you will be closer than ever. Or, and this is possible if you are still choosing partners from your old paradigm, they may find it is too exposing and will leave.

This is good news either way. If you get more passion and love and honesty from your partner, you win! If your partner leaves because they can't handle your truth and authentic expression, they will make room for a better partner to show up and meet you where you now are.

Your choice then is this: be closed and shallow with blame as your main means of expression or be open and free simply being honest and living authentically and enjoying more intimacy and connection with your lover.

If you are honest in your communications, in your interactions, and in your love life, you will be a whole lot more empowered and a whole lot happier. Sounds good to me.

Which do you choose?

Notes

Notes

Notes

ABOUT LOVE & ROMANCE

50 Ways To Love Your Lover

#31

Relationship rebound is a disservice to your new unfortunate lover & especially yourself. Respect and love yourself first.

You've just been through an intense break-up. It rocked your world. This break-up shocked you out of your complacency and your hurt feelings and pain are definitely in your face. You are feeling shattered, alone, insecure and hurt. Yes, you are feeling some grief too.

This is a good time to be in your own space, to allow healing to begin, and to do what is necessary to get back to being fully you again. It is a perfect time to take stock, to sort out what happened, and to do some healing of your own for yourself.

You are probably at your most vulnerable and raw. You are feeling pain and hurt.

It is also often at this point, where you come to a rather irrational and inaccurate resolution that the best way to get over this past lost romance and broken heart is to seek out love and another lover to feel better. And you jump in and immerse yourself in a new relationship as soon as possible.

50 Ways To Love Your Lover

Don't do it.

Your motivation of seeking another lover may be intended to calm and heal your hurting heart, as a salve for your wounds and raw pain.

However, that will not be the result. In fact, it will be far from the result you want. Yes, you may feel a temporary sense of euphoria, and even well-being. However, it will not last.

Taking this path will attract someone, anyone in fact, that you will use to help fill yourself up with good feelings, a temporary band-aid to your heart that still needs time to heal, to restore and renew. These distorted and illusory effects known as the *rebound* are not ultimately healthy or beneficial to you or to your temporary partner.

It may feel really good initially, however the effects are only temporary at best.

As I said, your heart requires time to heal, as does your psyche, and all the time your ego wants to get busy again and believe that everything is OK. What you really seek, and need is your own loving, your own self-care, and your own compassion.

To seek romance from this place is a very weak and lacking, and it is virtually impossible to find love and romance that truly fills you.

At best, it will be a temporary cover-up for your aching heart. At worst, it will deepen and exacerbate your pain and loss you were attempting to ignore in the first place.

Rebounding after a loss will ultimately not serve you.

You always have a choice. In love and romance, it is no different.

You can choose to look for love in all the wrong places (to quote a famous song from way back), where you will find a temporary band-aid for your broken heart. However, you will fail to find a solution to your pain and hurt this way. You will simply keep perpetuating the repeated cycle of burying your hurt and continue emotionally limping from lover to lover.

Or you can take deep care of yourself. Take time away from a partner, date, or new romance. Invest in you, and take time to heal your hurt emotions, and free your heart to fully and completely be whole once more.

Respect yourself and put yourself first. Take time for yourself, to love and care for yourself; let your own emotional wounds heal, be kind and gentle with yourself and steer clear of the dating scene for a time.

When you have been through this healing journey, you will be in a much healthier place, and be whole and fully restored to your natural being. You will be able to attract love and partnership that will lift you and inspire you, not just cover up the previous pain and hurt.

From this place, you can enter into a healthy relationship that truly is your desire, made manifest. You deserve respect.

Notes

Notes

Notes

#32

If you truly love someone, you do not need them to fill you up. Needing is lack; desire is opening. Love from your overflow.

Have you felt like your partner was the answer to your prayers? Did they fulfill your every need? Perhaps, you felt or feel incomplete without them?

If you truly love your partner, you will always enjoy them and feel connection to them, and it is wonderful.

However, if you need to be with them or have them around to feel OK, and are afraid of losing them, you've begun down the slippery slope to co-dependence, lowered self-confidence, and diminished self-support. Not so wonderful, is it?

This needy energy is coming from a place of being incomplete, a void that yearns for fulfillment. This is co-dependence. I did go into more detail and revealing about co-dependence and options for a better choice in Chapter #25 (if you want to read that chapter again).

Getting back to the theme of this chapter however, desire on the other hand, is to be attracted, to enjoy, to embrace with joy and excitement, and is not caught up in attachment or hooked into some sort of need for approval.

The feelings are very different and so are the intentions behind desire vs. need. You can feel internally how each is different in your heart and gut.

If you need someone, how does it feel? Compare that to how you feel in your heart and gut, when you desire someone. Notice the difference?

As Richard Bach wrote – *"If you love someone, set them free. If they come back, they're yours; if they don't, they never were."*

So, here's a reminder about who you are - You are a magnificent and fully self-sufficient individual who requires nothing from anyone. You are free, just as you are, there is nothing outside of you that you require or need to be filled up. You are unique and perfect, just as you are. Am I making myself clear?

The healthiest relationship you can have with anyone is one where you are already present to being filled full with your own love, your own self-support and self-approval and you bring that to your relationship. It really is that simple.

You give to your relationship and your partner from your over-flow. And they return the favor too.

Live and love this way, and it will absolutely transform your romance and relationship. You will enjoy more love, joy, and freedom than ever before. It is the addition of one partner's love, passion, and joy with another, rather than replacing or filling a void.

This is powerful and amazing and very likely if you want and desire it.

Do you desire it?

Notes

Notes

Notes

#33
True romance is sacred, profound and a pleasure on all levels, if you open your heart, do the work, and serve your partner.

In case you are wondering, the word "sacred" is not reserved or only relevant in religious language.

The word "sacred" is defined as *"entitled to reverence and respect"* and *"highly valued and important."*

Treating romance and relationship as sacred is very relevant to you having a powerful and authentic relationship. In fact, sacred romance is a powerful key to experience a deeply authentic and profound relationship.

How do you embrace and express sacred relationship?

Open your heart.

It may sound simple, yet it is profoundly transformational.

Yes, opening your heart might sound easy, easier than it actually is for you. With past pain, traumas, beliefs, issues, etc., your heart may have some shielding that is automatically in place to protect from further risk of pain and hurt. Which makes opening your heart less easy.

Many people in relationship spend their time protecting their heart. They are not opening their heart fully to their partner. They may open a couple of layers of their heart, and it appears they care, and love.

Yet just like an onion, there are many layers to your heart (and yes, sometimes there are tears in involved in the releasing and opening of them).

In fact, many individuals have some strong walls and barriers between themselves and their partners, built to protect and keep their hearts safe from hurt or suffering. These walls and barriers may be buried so deep, they may not even be consciously aware of them, let alone overcome them.

To truly embrace sacred relationship and deep connection, a deep level of trust, of openness and compassion is virtually a prerequisite.

It is indeed a deep calling, a profoundly healing choice to uncover and face these walls and barriers that are well established, comfortable, and believed necessary.

These barriers were self-erected for good reason, so it can be very scary and unsettling to even choose to resolve and heal the pain that required the installation of these walls and barriers in the first place.

However, choosing the healing path, and opening up these long-buried parts of your heart is so worth it. This path bears gifts of love, health, wholeness, and success that are truly worth it.

You will be able to fully open your heart to yourself (which is incredible on its own) and to your partner as well, with complete acceptance, peace, and gratitude for your past. The healing and wholeness you experience will transform how you feel, and how much you can feel and embrace.

Until you have experienced this, you have no idea how deep, how profound, and yes, how sacred relationship can truly be.

It is one of my truly joyful experiences to support my clients and audiences in this process, and to experience their whole and open hearts is deeply humbling.

If you have a partner who can hold the space for you, who can be your rock, your mirror, and your caring support as you transform your past pain into freedom and joy, you are blessed. Very blessed.

It is a powerful opportunity for wholeness and healing to open your heart anyway. To love beyond your past history and limits to a whole new level.

This is what I believe is a higher form of relationship. This is sacred relationship. And that is sacred indeed.

Notes

Notes

Notes

#34

Love does not equal chemistry. Love does not equal sex. Chemistry does not equal sex. All three can make your relationship amazing.

Chemistry is a great connector and attractor.

Sex is a powerful unifying opportunity (although for some it is simply a release, and for others it is an escape).

Love is a great transformer (and yes, there are many superlatives for love).

And they are very different, particularly in the context of romantic relationship.

This may seem to be stating the obvious, however many people haven't figured out that sex and love are different.

It is often chemistry, which sparks the connection between two consenting individuals that gets confused with sex and love.

It is the charge of attraction and magnetism that draws them to each other sexually and romantically (not always both though).

And to make things more complicated, many people confuse the *feeling* and *emotions* of sex with the *feelings* and *emotions* of love, so they mistake one for the other.

For example, an individual will profess profound emotional attachment for their partner after a one-night sexual encounter, and the other partner feels totally indifferent.

Chemistry can be fickle and short-lived. Love, on the other hand, is a state of being, a feeling that can endure and overcome many obstacles, challenges, and life altering experiences.

Love, as mentioned, is a powerful agent of transformation. Love will heal past hurts, love will reduce upsets and discords, and love will increase connection.

Love, in this context, is romantic love (*Eros*). Sex is what sex is – the physical act of, at one extreme "making love" and at the other extreme, "knocking boots."

Sex without love and chemistry is, to put it bluntly, just mutual masturbation. Is that what you really want?

Love and chemistry are different indeed, and yet they are both wonderful and magical in their unique ways, and together can make for amazing sexual connection.

One does not preclude the other. And neither alone is a good basis for a passionate and healthy romantic relationship. Chemistry alone may be obviously not the basis for long-term healthy and passionate relationship, yet love alone isn't the basis either.

Companionship? Certainly.

Romance? Passion? Not so much.

A way of explaining chemistry is using the example of magnets. A magnet has two Poles, North and South, and each pole is attracted to their opposite – North is attracted to South, South is attracted to North, they have polarity. So too the masculine and feminine are attracted to each other, as their polarity is heightened.

The power of this polarity is magical. It is often the motivating attraction between individuals. Chemistry is the initial spark of polarity – the magnetic attraction between two individuals. For some, chemistry fades. Actually, it is the lack of polarity that is happening. Polarity is the true attraction agent, and the good news is it can be renewed and rebuilt as an ongoing skill, when you know what to do.

The lack of this polarity is one of the core disruptions and discords couples have in their relationships, when the sexual partners lose their polar attraction, and they are left with being friends (without benefits). It is one of the fundamental issues I work on with my clients as well.

Polarity (aka chemistry) is the magnetism and tension that generates sexual excitement and attraction. It is very necessary for a fully expressed passionate, authentic, sexually satisfying long-term romance. And as I mentioned, the good news is this is a renewable resource. It can be maintained, recharged, and enjoyed continuously.

You will discover in later Chapters specific guidance about polarity, masculinity and femininity, and get deeper into this conversation (a little plug to keep reading). Let's get back to chemistry here, though.

Sex and chemistry are more connected and similar, particularly when you become aware of how sex ignites a chemical reaction in your body and emotions. Sex has an impact on your body that may surprise you - there are chemical changes that happen in your body when you have sex with a partner, particularly for the female partner, which can blur the lines between sex and love.

There are two hormones – *Oxytocin* and *Vasopressin* – in the human body that are triggers for bonding between people, particularly sexual partners, and in particular the female partner. Add to that mix *Dopamine*, which is a neurotransmitter reported to exacerbate this bonding.

These hormones and neurotransmitter are present in both male and female individuals, however women tend to have a different internal experience (meaning emotional experience) of these three items than men when engaging in sex.

This difference tends to create a greater tendency for women toward emotional bonding with their sexual partners. Men tend to experience less of this emotional bonding than women, so they are usually less emotionally attached or connected to their partner after sex, not surprisingly.

This difference between men and women has often been the cause of emotional pain when the connection is not mutual or reciprocated (such as the morning after). As has been expressed for millennia, women are supposedly more emotional than men.

To a degree this is true, and in this context, this can create pain and separation.

You may find this is your experience, or you may not. Either way, you now know you and your partner may feel emotionally different after sex. Be aware of this, and be understanding of each other.

What about love?

Love is the reason most couples get together, or at least, stay together. It is a great mystery on one hand, and the fuel that connects, inspires and uplifts us. Love heals wounds, including broken hearts, and is a powerful agent of change in people. Back to the "*Eros*" expression of love, known as romantic love.

Isn't it wonderful when you fall in love? Well, you might want to reconsider your language. If you want to "fall" in love, do you want to fall down, or does it feel better to rise up? Love up, not down. If you want to be in loving relationship, don't fall for them, lift yourself, lift them, be lifted by them, and fly in love together. Be in love with someone yes, however *falling* for them sounds rather painful (you might skin your knees!).

Yes, I am a romantic, and I am also aware of how we use and abuse language.

Love is a gift that must be shared, and sharing it in romantic relationship, with an intimate and committed partner who loves you back is profound and intoxicating. And some of that intoxication is chemical as previously described.

Being in love with someone does not guarantee great sex, or even any sex.

A powerful love connection doesn't necessarily mean a great sexual connection. They are not interchangeable in your relationship.

Bottom line: In a romantic and sexually active relationship, having both love and chemistry will launch your sexual connection to new heights.

Make sense?

Chemistry alone can and usually does fade. Chemistry sustained by love using polarity to renew the magnetic attraction can last a lifetime and will transform your love life into profound and passionate romance.

In simple terms, taking time to remember your natural state, your heart's alignment to your natural essence, be it masculine or feminine will deepen your connection with your partner, build polarity (aka. chemistry), and passion and attraction will increase.

I'll speak on this in more detail about the masculine and feminine in later chapters.

Bottom line: Enjoy it all.

Notes

Notes

#35

Love is the best lubricant ever created. It smooths the rough spots, facilitates deeper connection, and that is just the start.

Ah, ain't love grand?

Actually, it is. Love is magnificent, powerful, healing, transformational, opening, deepening, connecting, attracting, and so much more.

Love is the reason we get together in relationship; it is often the strongest reason we stay together in relationship as well.

Love is the lubrication system in the engine known as relationship.

Yet sometimes we forget.

For example:

Are you always loving when you are communicating with your partner?

50 Ways To Love Your Lover

Do you always listen to your partner from a loving space?

Do you feel your heart open before you share with your partner?

Do you remember what it was that attracted you to your partner back at the beginning?

Love is the core essence of relationship, and yet it sometimes gets forgotten when the going gets rough, or when one partner violates the trust of the other.

Love can sometimes be treated as something rather fickle, particularly when you don't trust your partner for some reason or other.

Yet, love is probably the best solution, the most effective resolution to heal upsets, restore communication and trust, and smooths the rough spots.

Love is even more than this. Love is a powerful force for good. Love is an incredible transformational agent that will cause us to know we are more than we previously believed ourselves to be.

Love deepens our connection with ourselves, and each other. And keeping love at the center of your romance, the core of your relationship is more than just a good idea. It is your best choice and your best focus every moment of every day.

Love is absolutely fundamental to have the depth of passion, commitment, honor, dedication, authenticity, connection, joy, understanding, compassion, caring, devotion, respect, and much, much more, that you have dreamed of in your vision of amazing relationship, for so long.

This Chapter simply reminds you of what you already know, both for relationships, and for your life generally. Love is powerful and profound and when fully expressed in relationship transforms and elevates the relationship to new and magnificent levels of intimacy and connection.

Basically, love rocks.

Notes

Notes

Notes

#36

Be romantic.
If you can't think of a way,
do a web search for
"romance" and "how-to."
There are so many magical
and tantalizing options,
explore them.
Often.

Do I really need to elaborate on this for you?

Romantic relationships require nurturing and active participation. Romance doesn't just happen; it develops with intention and involvement.

It requires active and conscious romance, from both partners.

Romance is an active process, and you participate with your partner in the act of romance. I think I've made this clear enough now.

50 Ways To Love Your Lover

The desire and expression of romance is not aligned with one gender over the other. Gentlemen, listen up. Both the masculine and feminine can take the lead in this. Trust me, whoever thinks of it first can be the hero to the other partner.

There are so many ways of expressing and sharing romance, ways of being romantic, thoughtful acts and ways you can be that give to your partner romantically.

You can do so many romantic activities with your partner. Yes, there is the well-known and well-used "candle-lit dinner," and also the equally well used "walk on the beach at sunset."

What makes romance and your love-life a whole lot more exciting and pleasurable is spontaneity. Have fun, and allow your creative juices flow to have magical and tantalizing ways of expressing romance with your partner.

There are so many ways to express romance. Romance can be expressed by a long planned and special event, or it can be evoked by a simple gesture, connection, or gift.

I'm sure you would love a checklist to make your life easier. Rather than insert a list of ideas right here, I have some suggestions for you.

I know you can come up with your own unique and original ideas to inspire and stir the romantic coals of your love-life with your partner.

Be a vanguard for fresh romance. Explore unusual and fresh ideas that will spark your partner's intrigue, excitement, and passion right back at you.

If you come up blank or simply want more inspiration, the Internet is a wonderful resource.

Go online and simply enter some basic keyword searches, such as "romance" and "how-to," or "romantic ideas."

You will very quickly have an inexhaustible list of romantic ideas and possibilities at your fingertips that will rock your partner's world (and yours too).

Would you like a head start?

You're in luck.

I have compiled a collection of over 140 romance tips and ideas and assembled them into an eBook entitled *"Adventures In Romance."* As my gift to you, download your own copy at **BarrySelby.com/air**. It will give you a whole lot of ideas and options in romance and joy. There are even more endless possibilities, right at your fingertips.

Go ahead and download your free copy of my eBook, and get started, get ahead, and get romantic.

It is what you really want, isn't it?

… Notes …

Notes

Notes

ABOUT SEXUAL ATTRACTION

50 Ways To Love Your Lover

#37

Men and women attract each other differently. Men see attraction, women feel attraction.

If you've browsed magazine ads, television commercials, billboards and the like, you may have noticed that sex sells.

It has been that way for decades, so I suspect you already know this.

In the more recent past, a lot of the media advertising and marketing sells sex targeted to both men and women for their products. Usually, the format of selling is visual - it is the physical appearance of the tight body and defined tone that is the media's idea for sexiness to both genders.

This is because the majority of people deciding on the ads, commercials, etc., are men.

Despite what the media presents, men and women are actually attracted differently. We have been trained to believe that women are attracted to men purely by how they look, the same as men to women. However, that's not how it used to be.

Yes, to women, the image of a strong man with ripped abs and big arms is sexy, yet it is not so much the visual image that is attracting her. It is the *feeling* of strength, the *feeling* of solid, reliable, dependable masculinity that is the attraction.

Men are visually attracted, which may well be the biggest understatement in this book. Unfortunately, the media has taken this idea to extremes and women have often fallen into the trap of attempting to dress and appear like their advertised counterparts. There's more to this, however, than simply wanting cleavage and rounded rear end.

It is fundamental to our nature as men to be attracted to how a woman looks.

Yes, what attracts a man to a woman is how she looks. Not purely her body, as many women believe and unfortunately many men unwittingly default to. It is also her inner light that shines through her presentation, her aliveness, her vitality, and life that attracts him.

When a woman gets dressed up for dates, choosing makeup, clothing, and jewelry, is her way of accentuating how she shines her light, and express her beauty. It is her light that is being decorated and emphasized.

On the other hand, women are attracted to a man who feels strong, who feels powerful and who feels solid. Men who know who they are, who are trustworthy, who are authentic, empowered by their inner strength and clear in their direction and purpose in life, are actually more attractive to women than a man who relies only on his physique and muscles to attract a date.

It is his depth and presence that feels stronger and powerful, that a muscular body can amplify but not replace.

Men and women are different, as is documented in several Chapters, and in this arena, we are truly opposites.

Women are drawn to men's stillness, presence, and depth.

Men are drawn to women's vitality, aliveness, and motion.

A man who stands in his stillness, his presence and his depth is deeply attractive to women. And a man who has direction and purpose (which is discussed elsewhere in this book) is even more attractive to a woman.

A woman who flows in grace, dances in her love of life, and exudes her lightness of being, her joie de vivre, her essential feminine nature is highly attractive to men.

Make sense?

Don't just take my word for this, check it out for yourself. Take a deeper look and notice what attracts you to a prospective partner. What is it about them that draws you in? What are they not showing that you know is in them? Do you feel closer to them, or more distant, attracted or turned off?

Check out other members of the opposite sex and discover for yourself what it is, specifically, that truly grabs your attention. It might be one quality, one aspect, one facet that draws you in, even though nothing else about them really does.

50 Ways To Love Your Lover

You will learn a lot about yourself doing this. You will learn what is really important in attraction for you as well.

Use this principle as your own gauge, your own guidance to learn about you.

Didn't see that one coming. Did you?

Notes

Notes

#38

We carry both masculine & feminine energy. Recognize your authentic polarity, attract your opposite polarity for your deepest passion.

You present yourself, your energy to the world in different ways, depending on situation, circumstance, and whom you are with. Your relationship partner, in particular, will be your best reflection and teacher for your energy.

Before I explain this further, here's some clarification.

Masculine and feminine is not your gender, nor is it about your sexual preference.

A man is male, and is likely masculine, although not always.

A woman is female, and is likely feminine, however not always.

Whether you are male or female, straight or gay, you have a combination, a blend if you will, of masculine and feminine energy.

To make this easier to understand, imagine a magnet. It has two Poles, North and South, which are magnetic opposites (no surprise) and are attracted to their reciprocal Pole. This means the North Pole is attracted to the South Pole, and the South Pole is attracted to the North Pole. However, a North Pole is not attracted to another North Pole, nor is South Pole attracted to another South Pole.

This is also true for our masculine and feminine polarity. Again, this is not about gender preference or sexual preference; the magnet analogy corresponds to the masculine and feminine energy you express, not your sexual preference and not your gender.

And to make things more interesting, it is not necessarily tied to the male or female form. A heterosexual man can be more centered in his feminine polarity than masculine (such as a care giver), just as a heterosexual woman can be more centered in her masculine polarity than feminine (such as a police officer).

This is not about straight or gay relationships, it is about the attraction of who we are innately and what we present, our masculine and/or feminine polarity.

Most individuals embody of a combination of masculine and feminine energy (for want of a better word). People are rarely all masculine or all feminine in their polarity; they have a blend of both. And important to know, your polarity is not fixed forever, it can be changed, or change innately.

More on that in a minute.

First a warning: To explain this blend and balance of polarity and energy, I will be using percentages to describe this most effectively. This is simple addition, not complex mathematics, algebra, or calculus, so please relax.

We are whole individuals, obviously, and our energy, our polarity is a combination of masculine and feminine, which adds up to 100%. As I mentioned, very few individuals are 100% masculine (0% feminine) or 100% feminine (0% masculine). We are usually a mixed percentage that adds up to 100%, for instance, your 100% could be composed of 60% feminine and 40% masculine. Or vice versa.

An example: Joe is a regular guy in relationship with Mary, his lovely girlfriend. When we examine Joe's energy or polarity, we see he generally has about 75% masculine polarity and therefore must have 25% feminine polarity to add up to 100%. His girlfriend Mary, when viewed the same way ideally and likely has a reciprocal polarity balance with about 25% masculine and 75% feminine, again totaling 100%.

This makes them an energetic match in their sexual energy, as their polarity is opposite and matched – Joe and Mary's masculine energy combined totals 100% and their feminine energy combined also totals 100% of course.

Again, this is about sexual polarity, not gender, so this balance and polarity is transcendent of heterosexual relationship, it also aligns for gay relationship as well.

So far, so good.

There are instances in heterosexual relationship where each partners' sexual polarity does not align with their gender. Using our example couple from earlier, Joe could be more in his feminine than his masculine polarity and Mary more in her masculine and less in her feminine. This is still a sexually attracted couple, and some heterosexual couples enjoy their relationship this way, *if* the energy balance is naturally this way.

If, however, an individual has adopted a different masculine/feminine polarity that does not match their natural innate balance, due to some past influence or even trauma, they will not fully blossom in relationship. That is until they heal that past trauma and reconnect and align with their authentic and natural sexual polarity.

This person would need an understanding and caring partner to both shift and balance them as they journey back to and ultimately remember their natural balance.

Or they would choose to do this healing work while they are single, which will shift who they will be attracted to when they seek a new relationship.

So far, I have been describing the relationship polarity relative to sexual attraction.

To make things more interesting, in day to day living, most individuals do not have a fixed point of balance in their polarity. In actuality, their blend of masculine and feminine polarity will vary depending on circumstance and need.

For example, a single person (regardless of gender and natural polarity) would be more in their masculine polarity when getting things done; accomplishing tasks, etc., working in an office, or operating machinery, even driving generally requires a more masculine presence.

Then, that same single person would be more in their feminine when they are being compassionate to someone, or nurturing a baby, etc.

Now combine two such individuals into a relationship, and you will realize there are times when both partners would be in their masculine polarity at the same time, for example, taking care of the bills, getting things done, etc. At another moment, they could be in their feminine polarity at the same time when, for example, they are nurturing a baby.

In romantic relationship, after time together, especially years, the sexual tension and chemistry between partners may be somewhat diminished, understandably.

Understanding this polarity balance of your human make-up, you see how there can be more attraction and sexual chemistry when one partner is fully embodying their masculine polarity and the other partner is fully residing in their feminine polarity.

Simply said, the more *extreme* your polarity with your partner, the stronger the attraction between masculine and feminine (like the North and South poles on the magnet), the deeper the passion and sexual connection.

Knowing that you have this variability in your sexual connection, you can make choices to magnify and generate more polarity between you when you choose to engage sexually. There are activities, intentions and processes you can do to regenerate your sexual chemistry with your partner. I teach a few to my clients and audience.

I hope you take this to heart. You deserve and can have a fully expressing inter-dependent relationship that is 100/100, basically 200% in this context.

As mentioned, each person expresses themselves as 100% (whatever their polarity), two partners in relationship share a total of 200% together.

Referring back to the description and delineation of co-dependency and inter-dependency, if you are still choosing co-dependent relationships, you are existing in a 50/50 relationship, both are half-in. Neither of you are functioning at 100%, you will only be at around 50%, as will your partner. This feels rather half-hearted.

That's a lot less than what is possible.

You may realize, this is only the tip of the iceberg.

There is more on this subject in the next few Chapters. There is also a lot more information about this topic and its ramifications out there in books and seminars, etc. Check the bibliography at the back for some recommended reading.

Now you know.

Notes

Notes

#39

Connect and express your authentic nature, whether masculine or feminine. It will deepen your polarity and your passion.

As I mentioned in the previous Chapter, masculine and feminine polarity is not automatically gender aligned, although it is generally so.

For men, masculine polarity is generally the norm, however not always. For women, feminine polarity is generally the norm, and again, not always.

I think I made myself clear.

For the examples here, masculine will correspond to the male attribute and feminine will correspond to the female attribute.

In this Chapter, I will explore more about the differences and depth of masculine and feminine.

50 Ways To Love Your Lover

First: the masculine. Before I go any further, I'll differentiate masculine from macho, as they are, in fact, very different ways of being.

Over many decades, men have been taught by society, media, peers, and their own fathers, to stand up for themselves, "be a man," or "man up," etc., which meant was to be macho. What that more directly intended, to be blunt, was to stop being a wimp and grow some cojones.

This was and is a black-and-white view of the world, and at extremes portrayed a man as one of two types, either a kind and compassionate wimp (the *good* guy or boy) or a cutthroat bad boy taking whatever he wants.

And for some time, the bad boy was portrayed as the one that excited his women the most, that ravished them (that's the polite way of saying it) then took off without a backward glance. He is a user and has no discernible heart, according to most of the media out there. All he really had was apparently large cojones!

And the good guys were the comfortable men, the ones who were loyal and unexciting, reliable, and solid. They had heart, but no daring, no dashing hero, and no backbone.

And that was basically the only choice women seemed to have. Thankfully, there is a third and more modern yet timeless man – the masculine man, also known as the authentic man.

This authentic man has been less obvious in the mainstream, although he has been around on the fringes, so to speak. And he includes the best qualities of both the bad boy and good guy.

Firstly, the authentic man is not all about his cojones (to be frank), he certainly has that manly aspect but not at the expense of his true strength.

The authentic man has an open heart and is unafraid to show his courage and vulnerability, knowing it does not make him weak, in fact it simply causes him to be open, compassionate, and honest.

The authentic man also has a strong and straight spine, which shows as clarity of who he is, ownership of his vision and purpose, his reason for being and he lives it. He has a strong character that makes a difference.

He epitomizes the masculine persona.

This, then, is the authentic masculine in full expression.

The feminine has had a few refinements over her female history (or is that *her*story?) to be clarified as well.

There was a time in the past for women to be empowered to succeed in the business world, to stop being the "meek housewife" staying at home, taking care of the kids, etc., while their husband was the breadwinner.

This stirring hit a high note in the 1960s when the Feminist Movement (also known as Women's Liberation, or Women's Lib for short) took hold in the Western World.

The premise was to empower and free women to be whatever they wanted which was welcome and long overdue. However, the execution of their mandate was less aligned and effective.

The Feminist Movement ideals virtually commanded women to burn their bras, wear pantsuits instead of skirts, take off their make-up, remove their big jewelry, and even cut their hair short.

Yes, women took more bold steps into the corporate world, and they generally stood toe to toe with the men in some areas. We won't get into the societal changes that occurred, nor the inequalities that still remain.

That would require a whole new book.

The point here is many women put aside their feminine polarity, so they could be successful in the world, and have forgotten it when it comes to dating, love, romance, and relationship.

Many women approached the whole relationship and romance conversation from the perspective of the man. Only in the past decade or so has there been a change to restore balance and polarity.

Yet, from what I have learned from a lot of clientele and friends, this behavior is still prevalent – women get stuck in their masculine polarity, and it messes up their love-life.

There is a time and place for women to embrace and use their masculine polarity, and in business is currently one of the most useful places. However, in relationship, unless the woman is naturally aligned with her masculine polarity, she will lose out on full passionate romance.

Put this woman (more in her masculine) together with one of the good guys (more in his feminine) from earlier. This relationship could work for a while; however, their relationship would be unlikely to fully blossom and succeed, as they are not in their natural balance.

For the record, I have personal experience of this particular example, and I know how challenging and ultimately unsuccessful it was, even if initially it worked, at least for me.

Suffice to say, men and women both have room to embrace and more greatly embody their authentic nature and polarity.

Now you have a reference regarding the power and authentic nature of polarity, here are some tips and understanding of how each aspect expresses and presents so you can align with your true nature.

The feminine embodies movement and light, expressing flow and grace, dancing in life, filled with joy and life.

The masculine embodies direction, clarity, and purpose, getting things done, achieving goals, directing and focused.

The feminine tends to have a wider view of what's happening, the masculine is more single focused to the exclusion of all else.

The masculine is making his impact on the world whereas the feminine is receiving and embracing all the world has to offer.

In simple language, the feminine is about filling up with life. The masculine is about emptying out and being used up. Feminine is movement. Masculine is stillness. Feminine is Life itself. Masculine is consciousness.

50 Ways To Love Your Lover

I am barely scraping the surface here, addressing the differences and strengths of each. There are also weaknesses to each, which is why we have both aspects within, so we can be more fully whole as ourselves and live fully in the world.

Refer to the bibliography for some useful reference.

You may see how you, in fact, do step into each polarity in different circumstances, and how also one of them is your more natural repose.

And as you read this, you will most likely have a sense of which is your stronger natural tendency.

As you recognize your natural polarity, remember this when you are relationship, particularly when it gets juicy.

Stay true to your authentic self.

Notes

Notes

#40

Ladies, let your man be masculine, and remember you are feminine. Don't compete for it, or you will both lose in romance.

This Chapter is particularly for you female readers (and for the men you love).

Ladies, from the previous Chapter you understand now that you may have adopted some masculine practices and habits so you could do well in the world. You might indeed be dynamic, powerful, and bullish in the business world, and live for the victory and the "kill."

For some men, this is actually very attractive yet not what is wanted in romance or the bedroom (at least not most of the time!). It can be dysfunctional in romantic settings, and can be disruptive to your relationship.

After reading the previous couple of Chapters, you may already understand the power and vulnerability of this particular principle.

In case you would like more detail, I'll break it down.

Ladies, if you compete for the masculine role at home as well as at work, you will lose. Not lose in the sense of competing to win or lose, you will lose the chemistry, romance, and passion that you crave and truly deserve in your relationship.

A healthy, passionate, and fulfilling relationship is best served with one partner inhabiting the masculine polarity and the other partner inhabiting the feminine polarity, at least when it comes to romance, chemistry and lovemaking.

Ladies, on behalf of myself and other men, please be generous and encouraging to your man.

Vacate your masculine persona when wanting romance and passion, and serve him by inviting him into his authentic masculine role (subtlety works here), and let him lead and guide.

He may surprise you.

Being in your sensuous and passionate feminine will excite him, it will empower him, and it will deepen him in his masculine heart, all of which will absolutely open you up to deeper connection, deeper passion, and greater satisfaction, particularly in the bedroom. Interested?

There are so many practices and activities you can use to deepen in your own feminine fullness and expression, and ways to remind you of your natural state.

You can choose nurturing and pampering activities, self-supportive intentions and actions that not only open your heart, they also reduce your masculine force into feminine softness, and allow you to fully embody your feminine self.

There are simple and pleasurable actions, like taking a bubble bath with candles and soft music, or even spa treatments and more invested self-nurturing activities. Spending time with other women sharing in sisterhood can be the catalyst to restore you back to your feminine nature.

You can choose powerful feminine expression and excitement that will polarize his response to you and turn up the juice.

There are exercise classes like yoga or Pilates, dance classes to connect you to your body and get you moving, more erotic activities (pole-dancing, burlesque classes for example) that will reconnect you powerfully and sensually to your feminine core and power. Dance, play and move in grace, vitality, and joy, and fully embrace your femininity.

Either choice will add to your mutual passion with your partner, and you will powerfully excite and honor his masculine authenticity and he will thank you for it.

Be yourself, be feminine and love him as he is authentically aligned in his masculine. You will love him more and more, and he will certainly reciprocate.

Having said all that, for fun, I encourage and recommend you switch roles, once in a while.

50 Ways To Love Your Lover

You will discover new ways of enjoying each other.

Notes

Notes

#41

Gentlemen, do your ladies a favor: take the reins from their grasp gently, lead them in love and they will thank you, deeply.

This statement was a little controversial when I first shared it with my audience, so I intend to make this a lot clearer, so you understand what it truly means.

Now you've read the previous couple of Chapters (you have, haven't you?), you have a general understanding of the masculine and feminine as well as some of the differences.

If you didn't, go back and re-read them again, just to be sure.

I mentioned previously that women in the corporate business arena had, in many cases, adopted a masculine polarity to compete and succeed in business, whether in sales, management, or other arena.

And for some women, their polarity, for all intents and purposes, gets stuck in their masculine, and they do not connect back to their feminine automatically when they are with their lover.

50 Ways To Love Your Lover

That's putting it simply.

Sometimes it is good for the man to remember *for* her.

First, he is smart enough to recognize she is in her masculine mode. He then owns and embodies his full masculine vibration. Gently, and I mean gently, he leads his woman away from her masculine modality and attachments (email, business, phone, newspaper, desk, etc.) and supports her in remembering and connecting to her feminine.

For example, his woman gets home from the office, and he feels she needs support and love to realign to her feminine vibration.

He gently takes her coat and briefcase from her hands, as well as her keys and smart phone, and then leads her to the bathroom where he has a hot bubble bath waiting for her, with candles and soft light. He leaves her to soak and restore herself, and he will most likely benefit later on, from her restoration to her natural balance.

In so doing, he gives her permission and a reminder that she can drop back into her feminine and allow herself to renew her heart and her fullness, putting aside her masculine for another day. He also lets her know he has the masculine polarity handled, so she can relax and let go of it more easily.

The key here is gentleness. If he takes charge with gusto and doesn't feel into where she is, it is likely all he will do is push her further into her masculine, which is counter-productive to what the intention was.

Gentlemen, being gentle (gentle – man? hmmm) combined with inner quiet, calm strength and a smile will work wonders with your lady. Seriously.

This gift that men can give to their women (or more accurately, the masculine can give to the feminine), is a powerful and wonderfully healing opportunity for deeper connection and more passionate love. It will reestablish the magnetic polarity that feels so good. The feminine will truly appreciate this gift and kindness.

Of course, if these women choose to take a path of self-study, read some great books on this subject, or work with a great coach and confidant (hint, hint), they will definitely get unstuck, so to speak.

And their masculine partner will certainly appreciate it as well.

Notes

Notes

Notes

#42

Men will never understand women. Women will never understand men. It is the way of love to accept and celebrate our differences.

You probably already knew this, or at least suspected this.

Have you recognized that members of the opposite sex don't understand you, even if they believe they do? Or how you don't understand them to the degree you wish you could?

Men and women are different. Men and women generally do not understand each other, even though they use the same language. Words and statements have different meanings to each gender, which complicates all communication.

John Gray made this abundantly clear in all his Mars and Venus books and teachings. Men and women are not wired the same way to communicate the same information to each other.

We are wired differently; we use language differently and that difference makes for some very interesting conversations and different perceptions.

To illustrate this difference, I'll present a light-hearted example, to show it more clearly.

Choose a color palette for a home, or clothing.

Men usually have a simple spectrum to choose from. A man might choose the color blue. A woman will naturally have a much larger range at her fingertips, so instead of one blue, she will have a range of blues in her vocabulary - periwinkle, sky, duck egg, royal, powder blue, ultramarine, and many, many more.

With such variance just in the naming of colors, is it any wonder that men and women have a whole different way of perceiving and describing life, experiences, relationships, romance or, heaven forbid, feelings?

Men and women also have different priorities in communication and emotional expression, which adds another dimension in understanding each other, or more accurately, *mis*understanding each other.

Here's another example:

Men and women generally prefer different choices for relaxation. The feminine tends toward a bubble bath, candles (you've figured that out by now) and chocolate, whereas the masculine generally prefers chilling out with the television, and perhaps a beer or two.

The reason for this is the masculine prefers relaxation by emptying out, whereas the feminine prefers to relax by restoring and filling up. We are yin and yang, direct opposites, and a perfect fit.

These are generalizations, yes, however there are many differences between the masculine and feminine. If this is your challenge, it can be a block to deeper connection.

Our differences can also be amusing, tedious or even confounding at times. And yet, our differences will persist as they are innate and core to who we are, so if you feel you must make your partner like yourself, give it up. As Billy Joel so eloquently sang – "Don't go changing to try and please me…"

Be authentic, certainly, be honest, be real, and be unique with your partner, and respect their authentic uniqueness, and watch the magic unfold.

It is in the embrace, acceptance, and celebration of our differences where the magic, the majesty and the magnificence are found.

Isn't this what attracted you to each other in the first place?

Notes

Notes

Notes

ABOUT LIFE
&
THE WORLD

50 Ways To Love Your Lover

#43

Don't trade your friends and your life for your lover. Dropping your regular life for your new partner can become infatuation, isolation and lead to failure.

You meet someone new; you fall in love (hard) with and for them, and you disappear from your regular social circles for months at a time.

You may not have done this yourself, but I'm sure you know someone like this. Or several people in fact.

You bump into this friend after a month or three, and they seem completely different from the friend you knew. They are protective and defensive of their relationship, and they will choose their partner over you and their other friendships every time, even to extremes.

They neglect their regular pastimes, social activities, and service commitments, perhaps even slacking off on their job schedule.

This is the way a person acts who is in a co-dependent relationship (described in a previous chapter). Hint: this is a sure sign for you of co-dependence, so you can make a change if it is you, or at least understand what's going on with your friend, if it is them.

Regardless of how this happens, and what the reasons are, the fact is this person has made a choice (perhaps mistakenly) of filling their whole life with their relationship, this one person (a very special person) at the exclusion of all other connections and friendship. This is a road that often ends in resentment and heartbreak.

If you are like most people, you have several areas of interest, focus and investment in your life. These areas would include health and wellness, social time, friends and family, hobbies, travel and adventure, work and career, money and finance, religion, or spirituality, etc. You will probably have anywhere between eight and twelve focus areas in your life.

If you imagine a wheel symbolizing your life, and these focus areas are spokes that enable your wheel to remain balanced and centered. If you were to neglect one area, one spoke of the wheel, your overall experience of life will be out of balance. If you neglect multiple areas of your life, your wheel and life would be drastically out of balance and would lead to imbalance and pain.

You have many areas in your life that you have enjoyed (mostly in balance I trust), and you have been participating in regular business, social, service, sports, and casual activities, etc.

These activities are what help you define what you love, what you do, and what you are about. Beyond just going to a job, you also enjoy a life that includes other areas that you take pleasure in doing. If you haven't been doing all that while you are single, you may want to get some coaching about life balance.

When you enter into relationship (beyond dating and first time meet-ups or hook-ups), you will make some room in your life for that relationship to grow and blossom. However, if you let it (or make it) take over and replace all your other life activities, the neglect of the other spokes of your life will be detrimental.

Being singularly consumed with your partner to the exclusion of all else is fun for a weekend, a few days, or a week or more. Beyond that though, this myopic focus is unhealthy both for your relationship itself and your life, if it is continued every day, week, and month.

Keeping your life moving in balance and expression supports your relationship. You can do a lot of activities together in partnership, and it is healthy and more fulfilling when you have time apart. Having time to be apart from your partner, so you can spend time with friends will actually keep your relationship fresh and healthy.

Bring your partner to your social gatherings and other places you normally go. Introduce them to your friends. This is healthy. It is a lot healthier than being a hermit with your partner.

Ideally you have friends you don't mind introducing to your new lover?

Be introduced to your partner's friends as well. You will learn a lot about each other, which will certainly be useful in your choices.

In fact, sharing your life activities, or at least a good portion of them, with your partner, and allow them to do the same with you, will deepen your relationship tremendously as it will show you more fully to each other in much more detail and variety.

50 Ways To Love Your Lover

You will discover deeper levels of intimacy and connection and perhaps most useful, a level of objectivity that would be untenable if immersed solely in your love-life.

Integrate your relationship into your life, rather than giving up one for the other. It is a healthy choice, for you, your partner, your relationship, and your life.

That's a win-win-win-win!

Notes

50 Ways To Love Your Lover

Notes

#44

Live your purpose, share your gifts & service in the world. You will attract your lover, or deepen the romance you already have, or both.

This may be the most motivational Chapter in this book, particularly for the male reader. At the same time, ignoring this principle is a relationship destroyer.

This may not seem like a relationship centric principle; however, it will have real impact on your romance.

I know this particular principle particularly well, and have suffered losses in my romance history by not knowing this one, having had more than one past relationship end because this principle was not in place.

Suffice to say, this lesson was hard won, after a lot of pain and loss in love, and it has forever changed my life, and romantic life, for the better.

In fact, it was the wake-up call that put me on my path to study and share this work with you, which includes this book. And of course, it is why this principle has a required spot in the **50 Ways To Love Your Lover**.

Let me speak existentially for a moment. Each of us has a reason for being on the planet. Not as a mystical concept, but a grounded and real part of living. We each have gifts and talents to share in the world, and with which we improve life for ourselves, and others, and to touch many lives.

These gifts and talents are expressed through our calling, our mission, and our contribution to the greater good.

For the masculine partner, it is most clearly defined as your purpose.

It is vital to your full expression and success in life to have a clear life purpose, a vision and direction and to be living it, or at least be on a quest to discover and embrace your purpose.

Let me be extra clear: for the masculine partner if that's you, get your purpose clear *first*. Be on track to express and share your purpose. Take action to have your purpose be real in the world. *Then*, you can embrace your romance and relationship at a whole new level, and not be of disservice to your feminine partner.

If you put relationship first, meaning being in love before you figure out your purpose, or even inquire within about it, you are likely to end up as a feminine partner, even though you are in a male gender body. You will attract a woman who is more aligned with her masculine than you are.

If you seek a woman who is in her feminine, you must be fully in your masculine vibration, which will require you have a direction and purpose to your life.

I know from my own experience how to not do this right.

For the feminine partner, your femininity and beauty is diminished when you are not sharing your gifts. You must blossom in your brightness and love by sharing your gifts and vision to inspire and uplift others. For you, this is not required *before* you are in relationship, however it certainly adds depth and light to your romance.

The gift of the feminine is the ability to be multi-faceted simultaneously, so you can be working on/in both areas. We men on the other hand are more linear, so tend to be good at doing one thing at a time, getting one up to speed then moving on to the next. What this means is for the masculine, it is most effective to have purpose first, then relationship second.

When both partners are living true to their heart's purpose and gifts, their romance and love deepens incredibly, and amazing things happen. The union of these two individuals is a powerful and wonderful transforming agent in the world. They touch the lives of others, and it is infectious.

The love each partner can share is magnified and multiplied in this vortex of alignment. Simply, it rocks.

On the other hand, if either or both partners are not living true to their heart's calling, there is an imbalance, a tendency for discord and selfishness, and a limited expression of love.

In some cases, both partners could be involved in the same expression of their unique and complementary mission and purpose. Often (but not always) the feminine will support the masculine's expression of purpose, as it in turn opens and fills the feminine heart.

This is a major key and hint for you to make different choices, and to align yourself with your inner vision and purpose, mission, calling, gifts, and find that also in your partner, so you shift your own experience and to have an incredibly vital, inspiring, and profound healthy relationship.

Not sure what your mission and purpose is?

This is important to your life, your relationship, and the world. I highly advise you take the steps to discover yours. Yes, I can assist you with clarification; it is part of my coaching work. Test drive my services with your first mini-session and find out more – **BarrySelby.com/chat**.

The world is waiting for you.

Notes

Notes

#45

Take a trip together within the early months of relationship. It will solidify your romance, or end it. You want to know.

"Honey, let's go on a trip."

If you are in a new relationship, does this excite you or put you in a panic? Do you feel confident this will deepen your connection and spice up your romance to a whole new level, or do you feel uncertain if you can be your regular self and comfortable if you go on this trip?

Either way, take the trip.

Before explaining further, I want to make sure you don't blindly jump in, without knowing your partner fairly well. Take the trip after you are committed to this relationship with each other.

When you begin a new relationship, it can be easy to settle very quickly into a certain level of comfort with your partner, and fall into a routine, keeping the same social interactions, connections, and such, being in consistent and usual environments etc. You become comfortable and settled in your relationship.

There's a funny thing that happens when you go on a trip though. You get to leave a lot of your comfort and usual surroundings behind and explore something different, particularly if you visit somewhere unfamiliar, such as the country if you a city dweller, or vice versa.

Just as being in a new relationship is a different place to be after being single, or different from a previous relationship that you have grown from, so traveling somewhere new will tend to feel different too.

What you will discover about yourself, free of your safe and comfortable environment and life, is what is most authentic and real for you in this relationship.

You will discover and reveal your true essence and your real self while on your trip, in ways you didn't while at home.

Taking a trip together, removing all usual distractions, will create a focus on the two of you. It will bring a much deeper level of truth and transparency forward, and you will know each other a lot better than you did before.

For your first trip away together, if either or both of you have kids, have them stay with a relative or family member so you can take this trip with just your partner.

This will be good for you, whether you become more closely connected, or if you in fact find you don't match after all. You will get much clearer about your partnership, and you will feel if you are aligned and willing to grow and deepen together.

Or you may find that you don't actually match as you first thought, and the connection you believed was there, in fact isn't.

It might feel drastic, however wouldn't you want to know sooner, rather than later?

The end result is you will either be a much more closely connected and aligned couple, or you will go your separate ways, and be available to a more matching partnership.

Consider the first trip and experiment in clarity and discernment for your future romance together.

It will be an honest choice and will save you a lot of time.

Consider this particular principle a time-saver and an express method to attract your true love. And you have the opportunity to travel to new places along the way.

That's a win-win, kinda.

Notes

Notes

Notes

#46

Do you have deal-breakers? Those things that you will not tolerate in a partner. Know them, honor them, and honor yourself.

In most spiritual practices, it is a goal to live a life where you love others unconditionally no matter what.

In romantic relationship, loving your partner unconditionally is a great way to love.

And it is not always the ideal.

Out of all the billions of individuals on the planet, we choose who we want to be with in romantic relationship. Our preferences help reduce our dating possibilities to a somewhat smaller number.

In romantic relationship, going deep and having an incredible connection is amazing. And there are certain behaviors, certain practices, certain habits, and certain personal preferences, etc., that you really want in your romance, and you would rather your partner matched these preferences.

And there are also behaviors, practices, habits, and preferences that you would rather not have in a partner. In fact, they will make your relationship experience painful.

For example, you might be vegan, and to be in relationship with someone who eats meat would not be preferable. Or maybe you dislike smoking so a partner who smokes would not line up for you. Or if you hold monogamy as a cornerstone for romantic intimate relationship, you will not want to be in relationship with a polyamorist or a swinger.

Being spiritual and unconditional might imply that giving up your deal-breakers may be a good thing and a high ideal, and somehow be virtuous.

As wonderful as that might sound, disregarding your own deal-breakers is simply disrespecting and ignoring your own wishes and preferences.

Ultimately, this can evoke resentment and even anger toward your partner, or as you become more self-aware, guilt and anger toward yourself (see previous Chapters for more about that).

Either way, it is likely not what you want.

What you do want to do is to get clear on your deal-breakers, and to make a list of them, consciously and honestly.

What works for you in partnership? What doesn't work for you in romance and relationship?

Is monogamy important to you? Is cheating a deal-breaker for you? If so, write it down.

Are drug-use, excessive alcohol consumption, or smoking deal-breakers for you? If so, write them down.

Keep writing down your authentic and honest deal-breakers that you know will not work for you.

At the same time as making your list authentic and real, don't become too finicky with your choices – for example, putting the cap (or not) back on the toothpaste is not necessarily a worthwhile deal-breaker, unless for you, it really is. Basically, be honest with yourself.

Once you have your list created, review it.

Are these the behaviors, habits, beliefs, etc., you truly cannot be comfortable with in a relationship?

Are any of these changeable? If your partner chose to change their diet to be vegan like you, or they gave up a polyamorous lifestyle for monogamy with you, would that work for you (and can you trust them too)?

If you met someone who met all your criteria and wish list in a partner, yet they also didn't pass one of your deal-breakers, would you be OK walking away?

This is vital – if you are not willing to walk away from your prospective date/mate who violates one or more of your deal-breaker list, either it is not really a deal-breaker, or you aren't being truly honest with yourself.

Personally, I have faced this one a few times, and in one instance, I tried to talk myself into ignoring a deal-breaker to be with her, as she was *almost* everything I wanted in a partner.

50 Ways To Love Your Lover

But that deal-breaker would not work for me, and as much as I attempted to ignore it, I couldn't.

Let's just say, things ended badly. I learned my lesson.

Get really clear on what is important to you in a romantic partner and your relationship with them, even the things you can't live without. Also be clear about what is important that you cannot live *with* in a romantic partner and relationship with them.

I speak from personal experience.

This principle will make your love life a whole lot happier.

Notes

Notes

#47

Know what is important to you, what your preferences are. These can make or break your relationship.

We covered deal-breakers in the previous Chapter. There's another level or layer of relationship parameters, which will make your relationship amazing or make it hell.

These can be called Preferences, however they are not to be taken lightly. These are really Essentials. This is the flip side of deal-breakers.

You probably already have a list of preferences. Not just the ones you want, but also the ones that are important to you, in your partner, in relationship and in your life when you next move into a committed relationship.

Trouble is, you have this all-important list, but then you meet someone cute, you forget you have the list, and you basically toss this list in the trash. Wrong move.

This principle is very basic and fundamental, yet many, many people overlook this when they *fall* in love with another.

50 Ways To Love Your Lover

Some items on your list are indeed negotiable or simply minor concerns when you are in relationship. They are either not impacting your life, or can be included in your relationship very easily.

Some of these items will in fact be deal-breakers for you if your partner will not or cannot accept or accommodate them for you.

Then there are the essential preferences, that are part of who you are, and for your relationship success, your partner needs to be a match for them with you. Really, these are your must-haves, because you must have these in place when you are with *the one*.

It may be a behavior or health-based item, or an item that supports you in living your life fully like having a partner who supports your dreams.

For example, you may want the same or similar spiritual or religious beliefs and practices than your partner. If this is fundamental to your happiness and way of being, and your partner has different yet complimentary beliefs, not a problem.

If however, your partner is atheist while you are strongly religious or spiritually centered, this would be more likely a deal-breaker for your romance.

Maybe you have a dietary preference that your partner can accommodate and work with. You might be vegetarian and your partner loves burgers. At home that might not work out, however if your partner chose to be vegetarian at home, and enjoyed burgers while out, that can be a workable preference, if it works for you.

This may seem pedantic and pedestrian, however, it is functionally vital to truly have a relationship that absolutely rocks.

If you are allergic to your partner's pet and no amount of medication helps you with it, that can really get in the way of your connection and openness you desire.

Trust me, I know this one.

And this is something only you can truly decide and own – some of your essential preferences that feel like deal-breakers, yet they are principles that you must have in relationship, once your partner understands and agrees to them.

Some of your essential preferences will feel like deal-breakers, and they will, in fact, keep you out of relationship with individuals, who either cannot or will not be comfortable with what you need.

This is interesting dance that relationship presents to you.

How much can you flex and flow, if you are used to being rigid and stiff.

Or how much can you hold to what is important to you, when you used to be overly flexible and be a doormat.

Examine your own criteria, your own personal needs, and your attachments to what needs to be.

Stand up for what you value and require, your essential preferences that will make your relationship rock.

50 Ways To Love Your Lover

You decide, it is always your choice.

Notes

Notes

ABOUT YOUR FUTURE

50 Ways To Love Your Lover

#48

If you don't know where you are going, you will never get where or what you want. This is true in romance, hint, hint.

It has been said many times and in many ways. In your life, if you don't have a clear picture of what you want, then you probably won't get it, nor will you know it if you see it.

And the corollary is: If you don't know where you're going, any port will do.

If you are on a trip, but you don't have a map or route of where you are going, how will you know how to get there? And how will you know if you get there? It is a challenge if you don't have a "there" in mind. I trust this is obvious.

Now apply this to your dating life. If you don't have a direction, plan, or intention for your future partner, don't be surprised if you don't end up in love. Yes, you might chance upon someone who you like and who likes you, however it is somewhat like playing the lottery, with little chance of winning the jackpot.

50 Ways To Love Your Lover

You are wise if you have clarity about what you really want when choosing what you desire in romance and love relationship.

This principle is not just about your relationship and romance (as are others in this book), it is truly a smart rule for living your life.

If you don't have a goal, intention, vision, or outcome in mind, in any area of your life, you will derail yourself from accomplishing much, if any, success in that area. You will certainly be less likely to achieve any measurable or specific goal.

This may seem rather mechanical to apply this to relationship, yet it is absolutely fundamental here as anywhere.

It is worse than a shot in the dark to enter a relationship without some intentions and visions of what you desire decided ahead of time. I call it playing "Russian Roulette with Romance." You are gambling with your love-life, and frankly, the odds of a long and healthy romance are stacked against you.

I think you get my point by now.

OK, let me ask you some specific questions in the area of romance, as that *is* the subject of this book and your interest.

- Do you have a vision of what your ideal romance looks like?

- Do you have a visceral feeling of what your ideal romance feels like?

- How would you feel after your wedding day?

- What do you bring to your divine partnership?

- What do you wish your partner to bring to you?

- Do you know what qualities you really want in your partner?

- Do you know what deal breakers you don't want in your partner?

You may have answered the last two questions from previous chapters. That was a hint, by the way.

Regarding your future partner:

- How do they respond when you touch them?

- How do you respond when they touch you?

- How will their hugs feel, how do you interact physically?

- How do their lips feel when you kiss? And what do they taste like when you kiss?

- How do they smell? Yes, how do they smell?

- How tall are they, next to you?

- What adventures do you travel to?

- What deep topics do you discuss?

- What beliefs do you share?

- What do you do together (apart from the obvious)?

For some individuals, this vision of the future can include a vision board, a simple and elegant device to create a visual reference for your ideal mate. There are resources online to guide you in creating your own vision board (I have provided a good resource for you in the next chapter).

There are so many sensory aspects and insights that you can imagine and vision for you and your new partner. It is vital that you have some sense of what these qualities and aspects are, so you have a reference for what you will intentionally attract.

One of the keys to anchoring your vision is how you feel about it. This feeling response is key, it makes your experience and vision more visceral. The feeling adds dimension to your intention, and it becomes more powerful and important to your mind and natural senses to attract that which you desire.

This works wonderfully for romance and divine partners. I use this with my clients to great effect, and the result is an almost magnetic pull to their divine partner.

And that is very attractive.

Notes

Notes

#49

Have a vision of your ideal romance? That is a great start. Spend time focused on how it feels, it magnifies the attraction.

Do you have a vision, a picture, a strong heart's desire or feeling, of what you want when you think of your dream relationship?

Can you picture what your ideal partner will look like? Where you will be? What you will be doing? Do you know how they carry themselves? How they interact with others?

What does your romance look like? Do you see yourself and your partner on vacation, at dinner, making love, growing old together?

Do you have a representation of your romantic vision? Do you have a graphic representation of that romantic vision? You will be ahead if you have a Vision Board for that very purpose.

In this context I am referring to that rather well-known, though often misunderstood and misused creation, the Vision Board. A Vision Board is a form of collage, a large poster board or similar, filled with images and words to affirm what you want.

The Vision Board has become a useful and powerful tool for good reason.

It is a powerful visual reminder of your goals, intentions, and vision of your future. Not only can you create a visual future vision of your whole life, you can also create and use these vision boards for specific area goals, such as health, career, family, spirituality, etc. And it is an absolutely ideal device to attract your relationship.

You fill a large poster board with pictures of romantic places, loving couples, reminders of romance, love, marriage (if that's your vision), activities and more together with affirmative words and statements that support the vision you hold for your ideal relationship. As previously mentioned, make sure you have a photo of yourself right in the center of the vision board to it makes the vision yours.

There is one additional aspect I believe you ought to take into consideration. There is a missing element for most vision board teachings, and that is the feeling level, the emotional trigger that will take your Vision Board from visual reference to visceral and emotional magnet that attracts what you want.

This, of course, requires that you have created your Vision Board in the first place. If you haven't, or have an old one that needs freshening up, this is a good time to create a current and attractive vision board that you are pleased with. I know you would love some handy instructions, so here are some instructions to get you started from **www.selfgrowth.com**. The language used is theirs, with some additions from me:

A vision board is simply a visual representation or collage of the things that you want to have, be, or do in your life.

It consists of a poster or foam board with cut-out pictures, drawings and/or writing on it of the things that you want in your life or the things that you want to become.

The purpose of a vision board is to activate the law of attraction to begin to pull things from your external environment that will enable you to realize your dream. By selecting pictures and writing that charges your emotions with feelings of passion, you will begin to manifest those things into your life.

The general elements that a well-designed vision board should include are:

***Visual.** Your subconscious mind works in pictures and images, so make your vision board as visual as possible with as many pictures as you like. You can supplement your pictures with words and phrases to increase the emotional juice you get from it.*

***Emotional.** Each picture on your vision board should evoke a positive emotional response from you. The mere sight of your vision board should evoke feelings of happiness and fuel your passion to attract it every time you look at it.*

Focus particular attention to images and words that evoke strong positive feeling in you. This creates a powerful and magnetic kinesthetic connection to both your vision-board and more importantly, your ideal relationship.

Strategically-placed. *Place your vision board strategically in a location that gives you maximum exposure to it. You need to constantly bathe your subconscious mind with its energy in order to manifest your desires quicker than you hope.*

Personal. *Place a current image of yourself in the center of the vision board. I highly recommend you use a photo of you that is recent, happy and smiling.*

This is vital to connect your subconscious into the vision and increase the attraction factor.

Negative feelings, self-doubt, and criticism can damage the delicate energy that your vision board emits. Place it in a private location, so it can only be seen by yourself.

Key items to be shown in one form or another (words and/or images) will include:

- How you feel and appear in your relationship

- What s/he is like

- His/her style

- What s/he brings to your relationship

- What s/he is about and up to

- And, very importantly, how your relationship feels and looks.

The most important component of your vision board is what it evokes for you, and how you feel when you think about it and look at it. Gather the materials you need and build this vision-board.

It is helpful, of course, if you use images that not only look like what you want to have, but also have the feeling of what you want, too.

Start now and enjoy the experience.

Once your vision board is created, spend some time with your Vision Board. In addition to simply looking at it (which you will do often), imagine how it would *feel* to embody and experience everything your Vision Board represents.

Feel into how it would be being with your partner, participating in different activities that have impact for you, and for the advanced student, project into your future, and feel how you are in a couple as you celebrate certain milestones.

Explore what the experience of living the life that is on your Vision Board. What would your life be like, how would it be different? Perhaps imagine your wedding day, or a special occasion with your partner.

Imagine how it is to come home to your partner, how your first date is (in the present tense of course), and how you are in bed together. It is your fantasy, go right ahead and enjoy it.

It is a potent and powerful tool, and it is a starting point I use with my clients.

50 Ways To Love Your Lover

If you knew how to add more magnetism to your future vision, and turn up the juice on attracting who you want to spend your love life with, wouldn't you do it?

Here is your permission slip.

Enjoy.

Notes

Notes

#50

Choose your beloved intentionally, every moment, and you will keep your love and your passion alive and thriving.

This principle is for you, particularly when you have been together for a long time, and the passion has faded. Actually, this principle is a great way to begin your relationship, then you won't need to worry about saving it later.

After you've been with your beloved for years, it can feel rather mundane. To be blunt, your desire for each other could feel a little stagnant. This will become your *normal*.

Normal in this context means your relationship has become rather flat, perhaps even flat-lined. It has stagnated and now feels rather boring, because ultimately it (and you) has lost passion (to say the least).

For some of you this might be your experience after being together for only a short time, in which case we need to talk.

50 Ways To Love Your Lover

If you don't take certain key steps, your attention and attraction can fade from the excitement, juicy passion, magic, and bliss it was when you were first together.

You do remember how it used to be with your lover, don't you?

You and/or your partner chose, probably without realizing or intending to, to take your romance (and your partner) for granted, and by doing so, you ended up sliding down the slippery slope to boredom and passivity.

A choice was made, perhaps unconsciously, that being comfortable was the default choice rather than consistently growing deeper together into newness, beyond what was comfortable.

If you made this choice that doesn't serve you, you always have another choice. This is the great news – you can always make a different choice. You have the choice to do something different that does serve you, and your partner, and your relationship.

First, and most important, declare your intention with your beloved. State your intention to respect them, to honor them, to embrace and passionately love them, and more.

Choose your words and your interactions wisely and with heart; it is worth the effort. And ask the same from them.

Second, remember everything changes, so each moment is different from every other moment, and your partner is constantly evolving and changing (as you are), maybe subtly or not.

You have the opportunity and joy to explore and discover new things about your partner, every moment.

How wonderful is that?

Rebuild the intimacy and intuition that was natural before, keep opening your heart to your partner, and connect to your own inner authentic nature, the deeper level where you drop the surface distractions and petty issues. Be inquisitive and interested in your partner.

Make your time together important, and sacred. Create a ritual practice when you connect with each other, which goes beyond the usual connecting you've always done.

Make love-making a special event, make kissing an act of conscious intimacy, so each touch wakes you up more and
more to your partner.

Surprise each other; ask each other what they want, and how they want to be loved. And leave the cellphones, laptops, television and other electronics out of the bedroom.

This is the core element for deepening your passion.

Knowing that there is more to know and open up to. Recognizing there is a fresh page on which to write your life and relationship story. Having a clean slate on which to create new moments, and a new evolution of your relationship, moment to moment to moment. This is a blessing, and it is also an intention.

Remember this truth, and your relationship and your passion will be deeper and richer than you ever dreamed.

And yes, you and your partner will thrive.

Isn't this exciting?

Notes

Notes

About the Author

Growing up in a small cul-de-sac outside of London, England, I was blessed to be part of a stable family with parents that married for life (my mother passed away in 2012, just after their 59th Anniversary), my father passed away nine years later in 2021, a day before the anniversary of my mother's passing.

I didn't know that life-long marriage was unusual, until I learned that others were not so lucky, as neighboring couples and parents of my friends were divorcing and families were breaking up. At a young age, this was my first sense that not everyone got along, and that there was more to successfully relating with others.

During my years in high school, I was the outsider. I wasn't part of the "in-crowd," I wasn't the cool kid, or the jock, or even the bad boy. I definitely wasn't the choice the cute girls wanted to go out with. To be honest, I was distressed by my lack of dating success (or lack of *any* dating for that matter) during my teen years. Yes, I had raging hormones (I was a healthy teenage boy after all), so I was more than a little frustrated at the same time. That, however, is another story.

Even though I wasn't the guy the girls wanted to go out with, I was their choice as the shoulder they cried on. I was the nice guy, the safe boy they confided in. I was safe. I was trustworthy.

I was their confidant.

This experience of being confidant is what most inspired me to learn about people and the choices they make in life and love. In fact, this fascination led me to immerse myself in over 25 years studying human potential, personal development, and spiritual exploration.

Along my journey, I have earned a Master's Degree in Spiritual Psychology from the University of Santa Monica (**UniversityOfSantaMonica.edu**), and I also earned my license as a professional spiritual counselor at the Agape International Spiritual Center (**AgapeLive.com**).

Geographically, I left England and lived in Germany and Belgium, before I relocated to the United States, California in particular, where I currently live.

My initial venture into the business world was as a programmer in the mainframe computer industry (before the days of PCs, laptops, and tablets). I was a geek.

Since then, I have had close to a dozen careers, including administration of a peace foundation, pre-press manager in the printing industry, professional photographer, Macintosh consultant (still a geek!), graphic designer, and now I am in my joy, passion, and service, as a professional speaker, podcaster, published author, relationship expert, singles' guide, and confidant.

I am not a very traditional person; in case you hadn't guessed.

In the arena of love, I have had my fair share of dysfunctional relationships and failed romance. I have endured a broken heart more than once, and yes, I have also broken a few hearts.

In this area, I was like almost everyone else.

In one key aspect, though, I am probably different than most.

I knew something needed to change, and I intentionally took time out from dating and being in relationships and took a hiatus of over five years being intentionally celibate and single.

As I mentioned earlier, I have been a student of personal growth and human understanding for many years. These past five-plus years have had a distinct focus, however. It has been my intentional study of the embodied authentic masculine and feminine polarities. I knew it was the missing piece of the puzzle for me (and it is for many singles and couples too).

Embodying and understanding the differences and importance of these polarities has changed my life. Learning and seeing how the partnership and polarity of masculine and feminine does and doesn't work in relationship and romance is vital and what I have become very passionate about.

This birthed my true calling and mission.

My passion is inspiring people like you to live authentic lives, and the vehicle that most effectively expresses this is my facilitation, leadership, guidance, and expertise with singles and couples to have amazing relationships, living purposefully and authentically, and fulfilling your highest potential.

Yes, I am passionate about living authentically, living from love first, and living to make a difference. My calling is guiding my clients like you to have powerfully profound, passionate, fulfilling, and healthy relationships.

I also consult with clients to reveal and share their gifts in the world. We all have them. Yes, even you.

I invite you to join my mailing list, so you will be in the loop for my latest events, offerings, and other ways of getting more out of your life and romance. Find out more about what I am up to, and how you can get more support and guidance at **BarrySelby.com.**

Find more suggestions in the Get More Section.

50 Ways To Love Your Lover

Bibliography
A small sampling of resources

David Deida

David has written many books on the subject of polarity and sexuality, including one of my favorites, about the authentic masculine – *The Way of The Superior Man*, and one for the feminine – *Dear Lover*.

Deida.info

Satyen and Suzanne Raja

These two are dear friends and authentic teachers and leaders in the area of relationships, masculine and feminine strength and passion. Their love and teaching has profoundly impacted my life, my heart and my own mission in the world.

WarriorSage.com

Alison Armstrong

Alison Armstrong is founder of PAX, and creator of her signature program: *Understanding Men, Satisfying Women.*

She is a powerful and profound speaker and teacher guiding from the feminine, understanding the differences that make attraction and relationship so powerful.

AlisonArmstrong.com

Dr. John Gray

World-famous for his multiple books, seminars and programs about *Mars & Venus,* he continues to share his wisdom and insights.

MarsVenus.com

Gay and Kathryn Hendricks

This couple is a pair of wonderful and caring individuals and teachers in their own right. Their many books and teachings have touched many lives, including mine. Among their many books are two that speak to finding authenticity and deep connection in relationship – *Conscious Loving* and more recently *The Conscious Heart*.

Hendricks.com

Colin Tipping

He is a foremost authority and author on the whole subject of forgiveness. His work is used in many organizations and groups. Two of his books are great resources to work through judgment issues and find forgiveness so you can be free - *Radical Forgiveness*, and *Radical Self Forgiveness*.

RadicalForgiveness.org

50 Ways To Love Your Lover

Get More.

I trust my book has inspired, and evoked some feelings about what you do or don't have. Additionally, you have discovered within these pages, some ideas and guidance to assist you in knowing what you really want, and how to attract it.

I'm sure you would love to share my book with others. You can buy copies for them, or simply refer them to the following link where they can purchase their own copy – **50WaysToLoveYourLover.com**

Invest in your own heart, your own journey, and your own romantic relationship success. You enjoyed my book, and now you feel you want more support. I invite you to take your next steps with me, whether that be with private coaching, my group offerings, or my online courses.

Visit my website and find out all that's going on and sign up for my newsletter at **BarrySelby.com** TODAY.

Make the choice to commit to yourself first, apply for one-on-one relationship support with me, beginning with a test drive of my guidance, by investing in a mini-session: **BarrySelby.com/chat**

50 Ways To Love Your Lover

May you live your life in love,
in amazement and joy-filled magic,
involved and inspired
by your dreams,
and your heart's desire.
May you share your gifts
and vision with the world,
embracing the love
you richly deserve,
and share your life
with your romantic equal,
enjoying and exploring
deep and profound
romance and relationship.

Barry Selby, October 28, 2011

50 Ways To Love Your Lover